What Is the Mission
of the Church?

What Is the Mission of the Church?

A Guide for Catholics

Roger P. Schroeder

ORBIS BOOKS

Maryknoll, New York 10545

Founded in 1970, Orbis Books endeavors to publish works that enlighten the mind, nourish the spirit, and challenge the conscience. The publishing arm of the Maryknoll Fathers and Brothers, Orbis seeks to explore the global dimensions of the Christian faith and mission, to invite dialogue with diverse cultures and religious traditions, and to serve the cause of reconciliation and peace. The books published reflect the opinions of their authors and are not meant to represent the official position of the Maryknoll Society. To obtain more information about Maryknoll and Orbis Books, please visit our website at www.maryknoll.org.

Manufactured in the United States of America.

Manuscript editing and typesetting by Joan Weber Laflamme.

Library of Congress Cataloging in Publication Data

Schroeder, Roger, 1951–
    What is the mission of the church? : a guide for Catholics / Roger P. Schroeder.
      p. cm.
    Includes bibliographical references and index.
    ISBN 978–1–57075–810–2 (pbk.)
  1. Catholic Church—Missions. 2. Mission of the church. I. Title.
    BV2180.S32 2008
    266'.2—dc22

                        2008023799

To the men and women of diocesan mission offices,
who animate, educate, coordinate, and inspire us
to take part in God's mission.

Contents

Abbreviations

AG   *Ad Gentes (Decree on the Church's Missionary Activity)*, Vatican Council II, 7 December 1965.

BMS   Baptist Missionary Society, founded in England in 1792.

CGS   *Called to Global Solidarity: International Challenges for U.S. Parishes*, statement from the Catholic bishops of the United States, 12 November 1997. See the text with handouts, resources, and suggestions, published in 1998 and entitled *Called to Global Solidarity: International Challenges for U.S. Parishes. A Statement of the National Conference of Catholic Bishops with Parish Resources.*

CRS   Catholic Relief Services, the international humanitarian agency of the Catholic community in the United States. Founded in 1943 by the U.S. Catholic bishops.

DH   *Dignitatis Humanae (Declaration on Religious Liberty)*, Vatican Council II, 7 December 1965.

DP   *Dialogue and Proclamation*, Congregation for the Evangelization of Peoples and Pontifical Council for Interreligious Dialogue, 1991.

EA   *Ecclesia in America (The Church in America)*, Pope John Paul II, post-synodal apostolic exhortation, 22 January 1999.

EN   *Evangelii Nuntiandi (Evangelization in the Modern World)*, Pope Paul VI, apostolic exhortation, 8 December 1975.

GS *Gaudium et Spes (Pastoral Constitution on the Church in the Modern World)*, Vatican Council II, 7 December 1965.

HCA Holy Childhood Association, a Pontifical Mission Society dedicated to involving children in missionary activity, established in the United States in 1893.

LG *Lumen Gentium (Dogmatic Constitution on the Church)*, Vatican Council II, 21 November 1964.

NA *Nostra Aetate (Declaration on the Relation of the Church to Non-Christian Religions)*, Vatican Council II, 28 October 1965.

OA *Octogesima Adveniens (A Call to Action on the Eightieth Anniversary of* Rerum Novarum), Pope Paul VI, apostolic letter, 14 May 1971.

RCIA The Rite of Christian Initiation for Adults is the formal process of instruction through which interested adults are gradually introduced to the Roman Catholic faith and way of life and, if they choose, led to baptism.

RM *Redemptoris Missio (On the Permanent Validity of the Church's Missionary Mandate)*, Pope John Paul II, encyclical letter, 7 December 1990.

SA *Slavorum Apostoli (Apostles of the Slavs)*, Pope John Paul II, encyclical letter, 2 June 1985.

SPF Society for the Propagation of the Faith, founded in 1822, an international association for the assistance by prayers and financial support of Catholic missionary activity.

TEE *To the Ends of the Earth*, statement on mission from the Catholic bishops of the United States, 12 November 1986.

USCMA United States Catholic Mission Association.

Acknowledgments

When I was asked to write this book about mission for Catholic parishes and dioceses in the United States, I knew that I needed some help. I had to shift my focus from the graduate classroom to the pews. Through my involvement over the years with the U.S. Catholic Mission Association, I had come to know many men and women dedicated to mission education, animation, and action. Within this setting I found a cluster of persons working in diocesan mission offices who were very willing to meet occasionally with me as a "think tank" for this project. I want to acknowledge and thank the following for this invaluable input and guidance: Sisters Frances Cunningham and Rosemary Huddleston (Milwaukee), Deacon Mickey Friesen and Mike Haasl (St. Paul-Minneapolis), Mike Gable (Cincinnati), and Rosanne Fischer (St. Cloud). On several other occasions the circle of "consultants and interested parties" widened to include other directors and staff members of diocesan mission offices who gathered in Milwaukee from a six-state Midwestern region. For three years (2004, 2006, 2007) I was privileged to provide input as a resource person for their regional gathering, during which time I also directly and indirectly gathered feedback and suggestions for writing and revising this book.

In response to my request in 2007 for someone to review the first draft, Mike Gable graciously volunteered to organize several discussions of the manuscript among some of his past and present members of the Mission Office Advisory Board of the Mission Office of the Archdiocese of Cincinnati, where Mike serves as the director. I want to acknowledge and thank Norma Colussi, Bob and Jane Friel, Joseph Mohlenkamp, Teresa Phillips, Peg Rummler, and particularly Mike Gable for their pages of suggestions, corrections, and affirmations. Their feedback provided me direction for the further rewrites and revisions. While I was not able to incorporate all the suggestions I received in the process of writing this book, I hope that I have sufficiently represented and respected all this invaluable assistance.

I also want to thank Bill Burrows, my editor at Orbis Books, for the initial invitation and vision and for his continual input and support, which was both challenging and encouraging.

What Is the Mission
of the Church?

1

How the Concept of Mission Has Changed

• •

An Introduction

From Ransoming Pagan Babies to Mission on Every Continent

Jesus was on a mission from God! God created the world and humanity out of love, but people unfortunately distanced themselves from God's love and from one another. God made a promise through Abraham, Moses, the prophets, and other holy men and women of Israel to reestablish that right relationship of love and that way of salvation. God sent Jesus Christ, who had existed from the beginning of time, to our world to show human beings who we are and how we are to live. Jesus taught us about God's love, which embraces all people, including the "impure" lepers and tax-collectors, which calls us to treat everyone as our neighbor and brother or sister, including our enemies, and which requires all of us as sinners to turn from our old ways to the new life of God. Jesus Christ was God's love, forgiveness, salvation, healing, justice, and compassion *in the flesh,* and he reestablished the right relationship with God through his life, death, and resurrection. Jesus was on a mission from God, and we Christians need to continue that mission *in the flesh.* People today search and yearn for God's love, forgiveness, salvation, healing, justice, and compassion.

For over two thousand years Christians have understood and practiced mission in many different ways. One of my earliest

1

images of mission comes from my Catholic grade school days in the early 1960s: collecting pennies in a little cardboard coin box to *"ransom a pagan baby."* I wrote the baptismal name a child would receive at baptism by a missionary in a faraway land on the outside of the box. My classmates and I proudly processed with our "mission boxes" to the front of the classroom. That was the understanding of mission for me and most Catholics at that time.

The why, who, where, what and how of mission in pre–Vatican II days were quite clear and straightforward. "Pagan" babies (or adults) needed to be saved from the fires of hell by the act of baptism that would bring them safely on board the church—that is, the *Roman Catholic Church*, the ark of salvation. The stereotypical missionary picture was that of a white priest baptizing a non-white person in such mission lands as Africa, Asia, and the Pacific. Mission was clearly seen as unidirectional, that is, basically from Europe and North America to everyone else. The missionary brought God to "those people." The twofold motivation for mission was the salvation of souls and the establishment of the visible church around the world.

New Understanding of Mission

Since the renewal of the Second Vatican Council (1962–65), many things have changed within the Catholic Church. The liturgy is celebrated in a language and style that promote fuller understanding and participation; lay people have become more actively involved; the attitudes of Catholics toward Protestants have shifted from competition and suspicion to cooperation and understanding. Vatican II likewise marked a dramatic turning point in the understanding of mission.

How do we understand and define mission today? Some twenty-five years after the council, Pope John Paul II in a key document on mission described mission in this way: "Proclamation is the permanent priority of mission. The Church cannot elude Christ's explicit mandate, nor deprive men and women of the 'Good News' about their being loved and saved by God" (RM 44). The pope wrote about mission as "a single but complex reality, and it develops in a variety of ways" (41). "The witness of a Christian life is

the first and irreplaceable form of mission" (42), and such witness includes a "commitment to peace, justice, human rights and
human promotion" (42). Other elements of mission involve forming local churches (48–50), incarnating the gospel in all cultures
(52–54), dialoguing with brothers and sisters of other religions
(55–57), and promoting development by forming consciences
(58–59). Earlier, Pope Paul VI drew the definition of mission from
the central message and explicit purpose of Jesus to preach the
good news of the kingdom/reign of God (EN 6) and also pointed
out that mission has many elements (17–18), must respect culture and the context (20), and does not always require words
(21). This last idea is captured nicely by the phrase associated
with Francis of Assisi: "Preach always, and if necessary use words."

Popes Paul VI and John Paul II and other Catholic writers often use the term *evangelization* instead of *mission*. In a broad
sense *evangelization* is intended to sum up the church's entire
mission. While there is a tendency at times to restrict the meaning
of *evangelization* to explicit verbal proclamation, a 2007 Vatican
document stresses the broad intention of this term: "In any case,
to evangelize does not mean simply to teach a doctrine, but to
proclaim Jesus Christ by one's words and actions, that is, to make
oneself an instrument of his presence and action in the world"
(*Doctrinal Note on Some Aspects of Evangelization*, 2). The term
evangelization in this book is understood as another word for
mission in this broad sense.

In an attempt to capture the all-embracing dynamic of mission
in a one-line definition, one can say that *mission is proclaiming,
serving, and witnessing to God's reign of love, salvation, and justice*. This working definition will be filled out as we proceed, but
this gives us a starting point. Now, back to the Second Vatican
Council and how it affected the practice of mission.

First of all, the church reclaimed its identity, from its early years,
of being missionary by its very nature in the Vatican II *Decree on
the Church's Missionary Activity* (AG 2). Therefore, every local
church and diocese is to be both mission sending and mission
receiving. The local churches of the "global South" used to be
considered the "missions," and now they are the most vital centers of mission. And the Catholic Church in North America and
Europe, which used to see itself only as mission sending, is now

in great need of what Pope John Paul II called "re-evangelization." Local churches, as a whole, and individual Christians of the North and South, are all part of the one body of Christ, and therefore they should relate to and work with one another with mutual respect. It is no longer a one-way relationship.

Second, the church recognized that God was and is somehow also present in other religions, non-Western cultures, and in the world and society in general. The mysterious and wonderful movement of God's spirit, like the wind, cannot be captured within church walls or certain geographical territories. Within this context we must shift from the old heroic, paternalistic model of mission—reaching down to "save" and "help" another person—to a model of humility and mutuality—developing a reciprocal relationship out of respect for how God is already present in the other.

These two changes in understanding challenge those deep and dangerous attitudes that see mission efforts as some type of church foreign-aid program. It is not the "rich" of the North helping the "poor" of the South. In other words, attitudes of paternalism and superiority are to be replaced by mutuality and respect. Each local church and individual in mission is enriched through the others. In this ongoing relationship and process, everyone is called to conversion from the "old ways" to the "new ways" to be in right relationship with God and God's world. This understanding of mission since the Second Vatican Council does not discredit the good accomplished by the many committed and well-intentioned Christians and missionaries of the past. However, just as the church has changed over time to remain faithful to God's call in new situations, there is a call for new attitudes and approaches as God's Spirit leads the church into today's world.

Pope John Paul II affirmed that "there is a new awareness that missionary activity is a matter for all Christians, for all dioceses and parishes" (RM 2). A few years earlier, the U.S. Catholic bishops published *To the Ends of the Earth: A Pastoral Statement on World Mission* to educate and animate Catholics with this new understanding of mission. How is this promoted in North America? The Pontifical Mission Societies, particularly the Society for the Propagation of the Faith (SPF) and the Holy Childhood Association (HCA), play a key role in this regard. For example, the activities of the SPF include coordinating the annual mission appeal with a visiting missionary coming to every parish (Missionary Cooperative Plan) and the worldwide celebration of Mission Sunday on the penultimate Sunday in October in order to promote mission interest and support. In place of "ransoming pagan babies," the HCA continues to find new ways to open the eyes of children to the larger world and to help them participate in mission. They particularly focus on children helping children. Catholic Relief Services (CRS) sponsors the Lenten Operation Rice Bowl program, inviting individuals, families, and parishes to pray, fast, and sacrifice in solidarity with the hungry and poor around the world. Religious and lay mission societies through their publications and other activities act as catalysts for stirring up interest and involvement in mission. Diocesan mission offices promote mission cooperation through their work with the Pontifical Mission Societies, and in addition, some have initiated and supported a variety of parish and diocesan programs such as immersion trips, short-term mission opportunities, and social justice programs. A number of parishes in the United States have entered into a "twinning" program with another parish either outside or within the country. Rather than simply sending money and prayer in one direction to help the "less fortunate," both parishes enter into a relationship of mutual support and participation in mission. Both parishes are to be mission sending and mission receiving.

The prayer proposed by the HCA in preparation for the third millennium closed in this way: "Strengthen in us our full-hearted response to our sisters and brothers, whether they live next door or in a faraway village. May we all be one in you" (1998). This powerful prayer for children highlights aspects that are foundational for all programs of mission today. Mission calls Catholics not only to donate money but also to be open to having their daily lives, attitudes and actions transformed by God's grace. All Christians—laity, ordained, and religious—by virtue of their baptism and through their lives, actions, and words, are to participate in God's mission of drawing all people to the reign of God and the fullness of God's life. The call of mission is not restricted to certain peoples or geographical areas ("mission lands" or "missions"); it includes peoples of all races, nations, and generations. Mission is not just out there but also in here. Parish twinning occurs both across and within national boundaries, and while most of the funds from Operation Rice Bowl support programs outside the United States, 25 percent is devoted to alleviating hunger and poverty within the country. Finally, these programs promote a sense of unity within the body of Christ and solidarity with the wider human family. These particular themes have been developed by U.S. Catholic bishops in their 1998 statement including practical suggestions for parishes, *Called to Global Solidarity: International Challenges for U.S. Parishes.*

Mission and Table Fellowship

One image and symbol of mission is a table. In many ways mission is concerned with responding to physical and spiritual hunger. As we cannot live without bodily nourishment, neither can we live without food for our souls. While we often do this on an individual basis, our most memorable moments of being fed occur with others. When we gather as a family or with friends around a table to eat, whether for a daily meal or on special occasions, we are renewed in both body and spirit. Praying during mealtime reminds us of this fact. All cultures recognize the importance of sharing food to maintain, strengthen, and reestablish relationships. Families gather in homes to eat together at the end of a day and during vacations; feasts are held to celebrate weddings, anniversaries, holy days, and holidays; villages, spouses, and friends share a meal to mark their reconciliation.

Around the eucharistic table we are also nourished, as individuals and as a community, by God's word and by sharing the Body and Blood of Christ. Jesus said, "I am the bread of life. The one who comes to me will never be hungry; the one who believes in me will never thirst" (Jn 6:35). Signs of the coming of the reign of God included Jesus feeding the multitudes and eating with sinners and tax-collectors. This latter action was scandalous for many religious authorities because it went against social and religious customs. The same attitude threatened early Jewish Christians who felt that eating with Gentiles was unclean, and even unthinkable. If such daily table fellowship was considered impossible, how could Jewish Christians and Gentile Christians share the same table in the "breaking of the bread" (Eucharist)? Facing and eventually overcoming this challenge enabled the early church with its diversity to share one baptism and one table as the body of Christ.

Time and time again the church has struggled with this fundamental Christian principle of gathering in table fellowship as brothers and sisters of Christ. Indigenous peoples of the Americas and Africa were considered less than human; Catholics transported and owned slaves; African Americans were not allowed to study in seminaries in the United States until the 1920s; Catholics slaughtered fellow Catholics in Rwanda; and many U.S. small towns until recently had one Catholic Church for whites and another for "people of color." In today's global village we are more united through communication, mass media, and travel, but we are more divided between the haves and the have-nots.

In 2002 the U.S. Catholic bishops published a pastoral reflection called *A Place at the Table*. It begins with a description of three "tables"—the family dining-room table, the table of the Eucharist, and the worldwide "table" of God's diverse peoples. The document includes the following from the *Catechism of the Catholic Church:* "The Eucharist commits us to the poor. To receive in truth the Body and Blood of Christ given up for us, we must recognize Christ in the poorest" (no. 1397). This pastoral reflection is focused on one aspect of mission: "A Catholic recommitment to overcome poverty and to respect the dignity of all God's children." However, this image of the three tables can apply to all aspects of proclaiming, serving, and witnessing to God's reign of love, salvation, and justice, if we think in terms of the physical and spiritual hungers of the whole person and of entire communities. It is interesting that Jesus' call to conversion was often followed by a meal together.

The parish-twinning program in the United States provides a creative, pastoral opportunity for developing face-to-face mutual relationships of table fellowship that draw parish communities beyond their parochial boundaries. Operation Rice Bowl explicitly promotes such a vision, expressed in its 2006 *Home Calendar Guide:* "Just as we celebrate the Eucharist on Sundays, we can use Operation Rice Bowl as a way to 'break bread' together with family and loved ones. We . . . learn about the joys and challenges in the lives of our brothers and sisters all around the world, and give concrete assistance to those most in need." Along with the activities of organizations like the Pontifical Mission Societies and diocesan mission offices mentioned above, one can think of local parish initiatives such as soup kitchens, neighborhood outreach, parish human-concerns committees, and peace-and-justice committees. Actually, who the church is and what it does is imaged as instrument and sign of feeding the hungers and thirsts of today, drawing women and men of diverse backgrounds into community, witnessing through word and action the good news of Jesus Christ, and inviting people to baptism and the eucharistic table. Pastors and parish councils, liturgy and music directors, catechetical leaders and prayer groups, evangelization teams and ministers of care, directors of the Rite of Christian Initiation for Adults (RCIA) and deacons, hospital and prison chaplains, counselors and youth ministers, Christian parents and health-care workers all contribute to and participate in drawing God's people to the table. "There is a variety of gifts but always the same Spirit; there are all sorts of service to be done, but always to the same Lord" (1 Cor 12:4–5).

Flowing from what has been said, we see that table fellowship is a powerful model and motivation for mission—linking Jesus as the bread of life with our daily life (dining-room table), our Christian faith (eucharistic table), and our relationship with people both near and far (the table of the "other"). This image will be developed throughout this book.

Additional Considerations and Challenges

While we have been talking about mission in a broad and basic sense as the responsibility of all Christians to participate in God's mission, at the same time we must not forget those Christians from every local church (not just from North America and Europe) and every age who are called to be missionaries. Their particular vocation to participate in God's mission in more intentional and explicit ways both near and far from home is an essential part of the body of Christ. The number of North American–born and European-born missionaries has decreased but these areas need to continue to support missionary efforts. The Society for the Propagation of the Faith is particularly committed to reminding dioceses and parishes about their connection with and responsibility for missionary activities beyond their national borders. On a worldwide scale, the Catholic Church and other Christian churches of the growing Christian majority of the South—Latin America, Africa, Asia, and the Pacific Islands—are sending an increasing number of missionaries within and outside their countries.

Other questions emerge in our post–Vatican II church and the world today. While we recognize that God is somehow already present in the lives, cultures, and religions of others, why and how do we continue to proclaim the gospel and call people to baptism and membership in the church today? What does mission mean for missionaries and Christians working and living as a small minority among the followers of other faiths? What does mission mean for those living under communist and repressive political regimes? What does mission mean in the face of poverty, HIV/AIDS, violence, war, starvation, migration, and natural disasters? What does mission mean among the street children of the exploding populations of our cities around the world?

Turning particularly to Europe, North America, and Australia, how can the gospel take root within contemporary secularized Western societies? How does the church reach those who are borderline Christians, no longer Christians, or never Christians? What about young people and those living in the suburbs? What responsibilities do Christians have in nations that yield tremendous political and economic power in the world? The recent waves of immigrants and refugees are changing the face of the church and society. On the one hand, they are raising new and challenging mission questions, regarding diversity, hospitality, justice, and racism. On the other hand, those who are Christians are contributing their own experiences of God and expressions of faith to the church, and many of them are becoming missionaries. What are the consequences of this changing scene of mission for individuals, parishes, and dioceses? Priests, brothers, and sisters from the nations of the South are now coming to the North as missionaries and church workers. How do they contribute, and how are they received? And, at the same time, how does the church of Europe and North America continue to call and prepare men and women, ordained and lay Catholics, as missionaries to work, short term and long term, both within and outside their national borders?

Aim and Structure of This Book

Although the external practice and devotion of ransoming pagan babies has disappeared, the common understanding of mission is still often tied to such pre–Vatican II images. Television, movies, novels, and even some missionary magazines continue to reinforce the more paternalistic idea of mission. Many Catholics with this understanding continue to support missionary work, no matter how it is carried out in reality. Other Catholics question the purpose of mission because they continue mistakenly to identify mission with approaches that basically forced or enticed people to become Christians. A third group is not concerned at all about mission. Finally, some Catholics are aware, to various degrees, of the changing face of mission, and they are interested and engaged in the challenge and potential it offers. Where do you find yourself? This book is intended for all four audiences. It provides the framework for understanding the ideal and practice of mission since the Second Vatican Council and for addressing the questions that were raised above as well as other issues. This will be quite new for many, while simply filling in gaps for others. It is hoped that these pages will also inspire you to action.

This work attempts to be comprehensive without too much detail and concise without being overly simplified. After this Introduction, Chapter 2 describes the origins of mission in God and how this is seen in the Spirit, Jesus Christ, and the reign of God. Chapter 3 describes how early Christians carried out this mission beyond Jerusalem, as portrayed in the Acts of the Apostles. Chapters 4 and 5 provide a series of snapshots of the variety of ways in which mission has actually been done from the early church until the twentieth century and what lessons we can learn for today. Building upon the ground work of the first five chapters, the next three chapters spell out the understanding of mission since the Second Vatican Council. Chapter 6 focuses on the why, who, and where of mission; Chapter 7 on the what of mission; and Chapter 8 on the spirituality and the practice (how) of mission. This final chapter points to specific parish and diocesan resources with down-to-earth examples and suggestions. At the end of every chapter there are suggested questions and reflections as well as further readings to guide you through this process to the next step: what mission can mean practically for you, your family, your parish, and your diocese. Two appendices with pastoral resources and an extended bibliography are included at the end. Overall, these chapters provide what is stated in the subtitle of this book: *A Guide for Catholics.*

On one level, this book will satisfy your mind by providing you with a better theological and historical understanding of mission— what it has meant in the past and especially what it means in the present. On a second level, reading these pages will nourish your heart through personal reflection on how God continues to offer you, the church, and the world that bread of life. Third, the book provides a guide and practical tools for doing mission in your parish and diocese. Finally, these printed words may inspire you to committed action for God's mission of drawing people into table fellowship. Jesus responded with love and compassion to so many hungry and searching people and called them to conversion and a fuller life in God, and we are to do the same—around our table at home, the eucharistic table, and the table of the "other."

Questions for Reflection

1. In terms of mission awareness and activity, what has been your experience of parish twinning, Operation Rice Bowl, or the annual mission appeal?
2. In which of the four groups—"old"-style supporters, those who question the purpose of mission, the disinterested, or the engaged—would you put yourself?
3. What is the most immediate question about mission that you want to have answered?

Suggestions for Further Reading

Bellagamba, Anthony. *Mission and Ministry in the Global Church.* Maryknoll, NY: Orbis Books, 1992. Chapter 1. Overview of current mission trends by an experienced missionary in Africa.

Bosch, David J. "The Vulnerability of Mission." In *New Directions in Mission and Evangelization 2*, ed. James A. Scherer and Stephen B. Bevans, 73–86. Maryknoll, NY: Orbis Books, 1994. Insightful and moving description of the shift in mission perspective and approach.

Gittins, Anthony. "Mission: What's It Got to Do with Me?" *The Living Light* 34, no. 3 (Spring 1998): 6–13. Entire issue of this publication of short popular articles by the Department of Education of the United States Catholic Conference is on the theme "Mission and Missions."

National Conference of Catholic Bishops. *To the Ends of the Earth: A Pastoral Statement on World Mission*. Washington, DC: USCC, 1986. Paragraphs 1–21. Introduction and first section, "The New Missionary Context," of major U.S. Catholic document on mission.

2

Starting with the Big Picture

• •

God's Mission, the Reign of God,
and Christ the Savior

The word *mission* has often been associated with baptisms and building churches. While this is a part of mission, such a *starting point* for mission could and has led to misunderstandings and even blunders in our Christian history. One of the key insights of the Second Vatican Council was to reaffirm that not only the starting point of mission and church (and, of course, the meaning of life) but also the end point is always with God. Where did we come from and where are we going? Although the church certainly never denied this, there has been the tendency over time to overemphasize the goals of the institutional church or individual missionaries and to forget the "big picture." All things are ultimately about God's plan for us and all of creation. God is always bigger than our image of God. Using the words of the African American ex-slave Sojourner Truth: "Oh, God, I did not know you were so big" (Truth 1996, 173).

We begin this chapter by remembering the big picture, reflecting with the eyes of faith on how God has been active from creation throughout history. The Israelites and the first followers of Jesus played a key role in God's master plan, but in general they did not have the benefit of understanding this broader intention of God. In the Hebrew scriptures (Old Testament), the Israelites often associated Yahweh's plan with material success (in battles, acquiring land, and daily living) for themselves only, although the universal mission did surface on occasion. Most people who

13

followed Jesus thought that he would establish an earthly kingdom. It was only later, in reflecting on the life, death, and resurrection of Jesus—that is, God revealed "in the flesh" and being
led by God's Spirit—that Christians were able to grasp more clearly,
although certainly never fully, the mysterious and wonderful plan
of God. This is where we start.

God's Mission and the Spirit

Already at creation we find all three Persons of the Trinity.
God created heaven and earth (Gn 1:1); God's Spirit (wind) hovered over the waters (Gn 1:2); and the Word was with God and
through the Word "all things came into being" (Jn 1:3). Humanity was created in God's image and likeness, and in looking upon
all of creation, God saw that all of it was very good (Gn 1:31).
According to the imagery of Genesis, human beings (Adam and
Eve) in the beginning found themselves within the luscious Garden of Eden, but with their free wills they succumbed to evil and
forfeited the fullness of life that God had intended for them. The
story of Cain and Abel indicates that soon people did not recognize and respect the image of God in one another. However, God
did not abandon humanity. Through faith-filled people like
Abraham and Sarah, Isaac and Jacob, Moses and Aaron, God
maintained a particular relationship with the Jewish people, reaf-
firming them over and over again as they periodically turned away
from God. God's Spirit called—through the voices of prophets;
through the words of the psalms, proverbs, and wisdom literature; and through the lives of holy men and women—the people
to repent and return to God.

This relationship or covenant with the chosen people was intended as a part of God's plan to draw all nations to God. In a
mysterious and constant movement God's Spirit from the beginning of time was also stirring within the histories, cultures, and
even the religions of all peoples. The Word, which was God and
existed with God from the beginning, became flesh in Jesus to
fulfill this plan of God's saving love. The Spirit of God was upon
Jesus at his baptism and throughout his life and ministry as the
words of the prophet Isaiah were fulfilled: "The Spirit of the Lord

is upon me, because he has anointed me to bring glad tidings to the poor" (Is 61:1a; Lk 4:18a). In Christ, God is revealed as calling all people to greater and more abundant life both now and in the life to come.

The Second Vatican Council in its *Decree on the Church's Missionary Activity* offered a beautiful description of this interwoven movement of each Person of the Trinity in the divine plan, the *mission of God*. God the Father, like an overflowing and life-giving fountain of love (AG 2), created the world and called humanity to share in the fullness of God's life. God has shown this self-giving and self-revealing nature concretely in Jesus Christ and throughout history through the Spirit (AG 3–4). God's mission is an ebb-and-flow movement of saving love, from God and back to God. According to British missiologist Anthony Gittins, mission is God's job description, capturing "both what God does and who God is" (Gittins 1998, 8). Following up on this, the church exists only as a result of and for the sake of God's mission—that over-flowing fountain of love that is working outside the boundaries of the church as well. All peoples are made in God's image and are to reflect this self-giving love of God. Jesus showed us concretely what this means.

Jesus and the Reign of God

Jesus, as divine and human, had such a close relationship with God that in his prayer he called God by the affectionate term *Abba*, which was almost like calling God "Daddy." This shocked many people because they thought of God more as a distant judge. One of the most powerful images of God comes to us through Jesus' parable of the prodigal son (Lk 15:11–32). God is like the forgiving father—always loving, patient, and ready to forgive—looking out to the horizon and waiting for the lost child to return home. Jesus also knew that God's love is inclusive of all peoples, not limited to the Jewish people. God's desire is that all people be saved from the bonds of sin and share in the fullness of God's life.

Jesus' central message was "Repent, for the kingdom of heaven is close at hand" (Mt 4:17). Everything that Jesus was and did was focused on preaching, serving, and witnessing to this kingdom or reign of God. Jesus *preached* and described this reign through parables, short and vivid stories that continue to be retold today. Who can forget the image of the shepherd searching for the lost sheep, the tiny mustard seed growing into a tree, the merchant finding the pearl of great value, or the candle that is not to be hidden but rather to be put on the lamp stand so that all may see the light? Jesus *served* the reign of God through his exorcisms and healings (sometimes including the forgiveness of sins), which showed that the loving God is near and wants people to be freed from all forms of evil and suffering. Furthermore, through his association with women and those on the edges of society and his table fellowship with tax-collectors and those considered sinners, Jesus *witnessed* to an inclusive reign of God that invited God's sons and daughters into a new relationship with God and one another. In this way Jesus lived out the words of Isaiah that he read at the beginning of his ministry in Nazareth: "The spirit of the Lord is upon me; therefore, he has anointed me. He has sent me to bring glad tidings to the poor, to proclaim liberty to captives.... To announce a year of favor from the Lord" (Lk 4:18–19). Jesus' total commitment to God's mission would lead to his suffering, death, and ultimately his resurrection.

Ten years after the end of the Second Vatican Council, Pope Paul VI published the apostolic exhortation entitled *Evangelization in the Modern World*. This church teaching bases the understanding of mission on Jesus Christ and the reign of God, pointing out that Jesus is the "first and greatest evangelizer" (EN 7) and that the purpose of the church is to prolong and continue this mission of Jesus (EN 15). In a very strong statement, the pope insists that the proclamation of the kingdom or reign of God "is so important that, by comparison, everything else becomes the 'rest,' which is 'given in addition.' Only the Kingdom therefore is absolute, and it makes everything else relative" (EN 8).

The Mission of Jesus and Table Fellowship

A closer look at the significance of Jesus' table fellowship with sinners and tax-collectors provides a key for understanding the meaning of the reign of God and mission (as indicated in Chapter 1). Throughout its long history, the Israelites were very concerned about preserving their own identity against external threats, whether they were a minority among other peoples or protecting their land boundaries. To maintain their identity and purity, they distinguished certain foods as pure and clean for eating and sacrifice and others as impure and unclean (Lv 11). On a deeper level, keeping these foods separate was considered essential for keeping order and avoiding chaos in their society, which is the concern of every culture. From the religious perspective, following these purity laws was seen as honoring God's holiness (Lv 10:10–11; Ez 22:26; 44:23) and as an important guide for their own holiness (Ex 22:31; Lv 20:22–26; Dt 14:2). Therefore, true table fellowship with Gentiles in terms of sharing the same food, wine, and even vessels was a threat to their deep-rooted cultural and religious identity. People were also separated into the pure and the impure. Besides the Gentiles and Samaritans ("half-Jews"), the list of those excluded from temple worship and normal contact included sinners, tax-collectors, lepers, menstruating women, and the blind and crippled. As we know, Jesus reached out to all these people.

The issue of table fellowship and meals in general is most clearly addressed by the author of the Gospel of Luke and the Acts of the Apostles. Jesus ate with the tax-collector Levi (Lk 5:29–30), allowed the woman sinner to wash his feet with her hair during another meal (Lk 7:36–38), and stayed in the home of Zacchaeus, another tax-collector (Lk 19:5–6). In all three cases religious leaders complained about Jesus having contact with these "unclean" persons. Yet, these three persons repented of their sins. Jesus explained that he came not to avoid such persons but to cleanse the sinner and offer forgiveness, as a doctor helps the sick (Lk 5:31–32), as a creditor pardons the debtor (Lk 7:40–43), as the Son of Man saves what was lost (Lk 19:10). Such table fellowship was a sign that the reign of God, whose love is inclusive, was at hand in Jesus. From our own experience we know that having a meal with another can be a moment of sharing more than food. How much more meaningful was this given the Jewish significance of table fellowship! In Jesus' words regarding Zacchaeus, "Today, salvation has come to this house, because this

man too is a son of Abraham" (Lk 19:9). Jesus' meal with him
confirmed that.

In chapter 14, Luke groups together several of Jesus' sayings
regarding table fellowship in order to challenge some practices of
the Christian communities to whom he was addressing his Gospel and to remind them of Jesus' teaching regarding the reign of
God. In the setting of having a meal in the home of one of the
Pharisees, Jesus teaches that the betterment (healing) of a human
person is more important than a strict interpretation of the Law
(14:1–6), that table fellowship should not be an occasion for placing oneself above others (14:7–11), and that guests should not
be invited to a meal according to their capacity to reciprocate
(14:12–14). Luke concludes with the parable of the banquet
(14:15–24), whereby those initially invited made excuses for not
coming and those who would normally be excluded—that is, "the
poor, the crippled, the blind and the lame" (14:21)—are invited
to the banquet. Taking these passages together, the reality and
symbol of table fellowship points to how the reign of God challenges aspects of the Jewish culture (and all cultures) that dis-
criminate against people based on economic, physical, or social
standards. Furthermore, these "impure" persons are not to be
separated from God but are embraced by God. Jesus witnessed to
this inclusive reign of God.

The story of the feeding of the five thousand in Luke (9:10–
17), which is also found in the other three gospels, portrays Jesus
as nourishing the crowds. The words "[Jesus] said the blessing
over them; then he broke them and handed them to his disciples"
point ahead to the Eucharist of the Last Supper (Lk 22:19) and
recognizing Jesus in the "breaking of the bread" along the road
to Emmaus (Lk 24:30). In the more developed presentation of
the "bread of life" in John's Gospel, Jesus warns, "Do not work
for food that cannot last, but work for food that endures to
eternal life, the kind of food the Son of Man is offering you" (Jn
6:27). John identifies Jesus himself as the eternal bread of life
(6:35–50) and then makes an explicit connection with the Eucharist (6:51–58). The link between table fellowship and the
Eucharist became a burning issue for the early Christian community.

Jesus Christ, the Savior

Over many years the relationship of the Jewish people with Yahweh had gone through many ups and downs. They had come to look toward that day when a messiah would finally reestablish the right relationship or covenant between God and God's people. Jesus came, and a small group of Jews eventually recognized him as the Christ (messiah) who offered them God's salvation. In response to Jesus' question to his disciples, "Who do you say that I am?" Peter stated, "You are the Christ" (see Mk 8:29; Lk 9:20). Later on, after the resurrection and Pentecost, Peter speaks of Jesus in this way: "There is no salvation in anyone else, for there is no other name in the whole world given to humanity by which we are able to be saved" (Acts 4:12). After his own dramatic conversion, the itinerant preacher Paul became the strong voice proclaiming "for us there is one God, the Father, from whom all things come and for whom we live; and one Lord Jesus Christ through whom everything was made and through whom we live" (1 Cor 8:6). At the center of Paul's life and preaching is the driving conviction that "through the crucified death of Jesus the Jew and in his subsequent exaltation through resurrection, all humanity was offered the possibility of moving from death to life, from sin to God" (Senior and Stuhlmueller 1983, 174).

About fifteen years after Pope Paul VI's *Evangelization in the Modern World,* John Paul II issued the encyclical *On the Permanent Validity of the Church's Missionary Mandate.* While building upon the understanding of mission as the mission of God in the Vatican II *Decree on the Church's Missionary Activity* and Paul VI's emphasis on the reign of God (in EN), John Paul II strongly affirms that "Christ is the one Savior of all, the only one able to reveal God and lead to God" (RM 5). Furthermore, "the Church believes that God has established Christ as the one mediator and that she herself has been established as the universal sacrament of salvation" (RM 9), which is an image of the church from the Second Vatican Council (see, for example, AG 7, 21).

We will return in Chapter 6 to a more in-depth study of these three major Catholic documents. They have been introduced in this chapter because they each contribute an important part to the big picture of mission.

Mission to All Peoples

If we step back to the time of Jesus, we see how people's lives were dramatically changed because of the mission of God and Jesus. Sinners and tax-collectors got a new lease on life, lepers and paralytics were healed, those enslaved to demons were freed, people heard a message of hope and a call to a new life and new relationships. Some became Jesus' disciples: Mary Magdalene, freed from seven demons; Joanna and Susanna (Lk 8:2–3); Matthew the tax-collector (Mt 9:9); the man born blind (Jn 9:35–38); Joseph of Arimathea (Mt 27:57); Martha and Mary (Lk 10:38–42); and of course, Peter, James, John, and the rest of the Twelve (Lk 6:12–16). Followers of Jesus are to be forgiving and compassionate as God is forgiving and compassionate. They are to love even their enemies, just as Jesus would forgive his persecutors. The parable of the good Samaritan describes how a disciple thinks and acts; rather than passing by on the other side of the road, a disciple goes the extra mile out of compassion and love for the "stranger."

Jesus' choice of a Samaritan (not a Jew) as the ideal disciple points to the boundary-breaking character of mission. Although Jesus devoted most of his time and energy to his fellow Jews, sign posts like this indicate that the good news is for all people, Jews and Gentiles alike. Regarding the Roman centurion, Jesus says that "in no one in Israel have I found such faith" (Mt 8:10). Jesus actually entered a house in an area occupied by Gentiles (Mk 7:24) and healed the daughter of the Syrophoenician (Canaanite) woman, even though she was not an Israelite, because of the mother's great faith (Mk 7:24–30; Mt 15:22–28); and Jesus made very favorable comments about the Gentile towns of Tyre and Sidon (Mt 11:20–24). Let us look more closely at the incident with the Samaritan woman. This moment captures Jesus in mission in a very intriguing situation. While it is not a scene of table fellowship in the strict sense, it is representative of Jesus "pushing the edges" of the purity laws to share not food, but contact, conversation and ultimately the word of God beyond Judaism. Jesus responds to the woman's physical and spiritual thirst by offering her living water.

Jesus Encounters the Samaritan Woman at the Well

The scene starts with Jesus, returning to his home base in Galilee, passing through Samaria. He is in an area that is sacred to the Samaritans because it is land given by Jacob to his son Joseph.

Jacob's well is there, and Jesus, tired by the journey, sat straight down by the well. It was about noon. (Jn 4:6)

The disciples have gone into town to buy food, so Jesus is alone at the well. A Samaritan woman comes to draw water, and Jesus asks her for a drink.

The Samaritan woman said to him, "What? You are a Jew and you ask me, a Samaritan woman, for a drink?" (4:9)

In this encounter Jesus crosses two boundaries. First, the Samaritans are culturally and religiously considered "half-Jews," and therefore better to be avoided if possible. Furthermore, Jesus as a man would not normally associate with a woman in these circumstances. But the mission of the reign of God is not to be constrained by such human limitations and categories. Finally, this occasion of mission happens in a very ordinary, daily situation. The woman has come to get water at the well.

Jesus replied: "If you only knew what God is offering and who it is that is saying to you: 'Give me a drink,' you would have been the one to ask, and he would have given you living water." (4:10)

Jesus talks about the good news in terms of the powerful symbol of living water, so that a person will never be thirsty again, even into eternal life. Although the woman doesn't fully grasp what he is saying, Jesus is speaking to her deepest spiritual yearnings.

"Sir," said the woman "give me some of that water, so that
I may never get thirsty and never have to come here again
to draw water." (4:15)

Then the conversation shifts, first to her personal life, to the
fact that she has had five husbands and the man she is currently
with is not her husband, and second to religion, to the question
of belief. The woman brings up the differing beliefs between the
Jews and Samaritans regarding the central place of worship. Jesus
and the woman are getting to the heart of the matter, to issues of
marital relationships and religious-cultural beliefs and identities.

Believe me, woman, the hour is coming when you will worship the Father neither on this mountain [as the Samaritans
do] nor in Jerusalem [as the Jews do]. . . . But the hour will
come—in fact it is here already—when true worshipers will
worship the Father in spirit and truth; that is the kind of
worshiper the Father wants. (4:21, 23)

These words of Jesus indicate that God gives a spirit that re-
veals the truth to both Jews and Samaritans. God's mission is
embracing people of different religious and cultural backgrounds.
And people are changed, made something new, in this process. In
the preceding chapter of John, Jesus described this to the Phari-
see Nicodemus in terms of being "born of the Spirit" (Jn 3:8)
and "living by the truth" (Jn 3:20). The exchange between Jesus
and the woman moves further into religious expectations and theology:

The woman said to him, "I know that the Messiah [that is,
Christ] is coming; when he comes he will tell us everything."
"I who am speaking to you," said Jesus, "I am he." (4:25–
26)

The shared expectation of the Messiah, the Savior, is explicitly
brought into the conversation. At this point the disciples return
and are surprised that Jesus is talking to this Samaritan woman.
Unbeknown to them, something of the mission of God has occurred at the well, and the Samaritan woman is a part of it.

The woman put down her water jar and hurried back to the town to tell the people, "Come and see a man who has told me everything I ever did; I wonder if he is the Christ?" (4:28–29)

Excited, she leaves her water jar, a possession of some value, to share the good news she has received at the well. She came to get water, but she got something else. She participates in the mission of God as she seeks to draw other people to Jesus.

This brought people out of the town, and they started walking toward him. . . . Many Samaritans of that town had believed in him on the strength of the woman's testimony." (4:30, 39)

At their insistence Jesus then stayed for two days. Although we don't know if Jesus ate with the Samaritans, the fact that he stayed with them is an indication of the boundary-crossing mission of God, which will be carried out after Pentecost. Jesus had simply intended to cross through Samaria on his journey to Galilee, but God's Spirit led him to cross over the differences of religion, culture, and gender to witness to the reign of God. And many believed.

When he spoke to them, many more came to believe; and they said to the woman, "Now we no longer believe because of what you told us; we have heard him ourselves and we know that he really is the savior of the world." (4:41–42)

The people of the town were drawn to Jesus by the Samaritan woman. Some believed due to her belief, while many others came to believe because of their direct experience of Jesus.

While this is certainly a story about Jesus in mission, it is also a story of the Samaritan woman, as a disciple, in mission—this woman who was willing to put down her water jar and hurry back into town to tell others about Jesus. In this story we also see the three major intersecting aspects of the big picture of mission—God's mission, the reign of God, and Christ the Savior.

Mission as Seeds and Weeds

Jesus not only witnessed to God's reign, but he also pointed to the conditions for entering that reign: "Repent, and believe the Good News" (Mk 1:15). Jesus recognized and confronted the presence of evil and sin in the world, and he called men and women to conversion. In this chapter we have seen that it was often those considered impure, the outcasts, and the marginalized who responded positively to Jesus' message. The parables that highlight this dynamic of good and evil and grace and sin most clearly are drawn from agricultural images. Jesus describes the reign of God in terms of seeds and weeds.

The parable of the sower and the seed appears in all three Synoptic Gospels (Mt 13:4–9; Mk 4:3–9; Lk 8:5–8). A sower is sowing seed, some of which falls on the edge of the path, some on rocky ground, some among thorns, and some into rich soil. Jesus later explains that the seed is the word of God (Lk 8:11), and the various contexts in which the seed lands represent the variety of possible responses by people to that word. God's word is offered freely for all with the intention that the seed may bear much fruit, but also in a way which respects humanity's free will to accept it or not. In the third scenario the seed is eventually choked by the thorns "so it produces nothing" (Mk 4:19). We all know that weeding is a necessary chore in any garden or field if we expect good seed to bear fruit.

A second parable is found in Matthew (13:24–30). It is the story of an enemy sowing weeds among the wheat while the farmer was asleep. Jesus later explains (13:36–43) that the sower is the Son of God, and the good seed represents those who are subject to the reign of God, while the weeds symbolize those who are contrary to that reign. While both grow together, the wheat (virtuous) will be separated from the weeds (evil) at the time of the harvest (the end of the world). Choices for or against the reign of God have consequences. Also, good and evil does exist side by side, sometimes very closely, as we know all too well.

While this is the case, another parable (Mk 4:26–29) reminds us that the seed, the word of God, will not only survive but will grow to full fruition on its own. "Night and day, while he sleeps, when he is awake, the seed is sprouting and growing; how, he does not know. Of its own accord the land produces first the shoot, then the ear, then the full grain in the ear" (4:27). The reign of God is *of God*, and the parable warns us against overzealous efforts to control God and others. While we are certainly called to participate in the mission of God, it remains a mystery ultimately in God's hands.

This set of parables on seeds and weeds forms an important part of Jesus' teaching about God, ourselves, and our world, and it provides an important part of our framework for understanding mission today.

Sketching the Big Picture

The intention of this chapter was to sketch the big picture, at least as well as we can from our human perspective. We place ourselves in God's world, which was initially created to reflect God's image and goodness, symbolized by the Garden of Eden. Sin and evil entered the scene, but God's love and plan were constant. God's mission of drawing humanity and all creation back to the fullness of God's life can be traced in the mysterious presence of the Spirit through time and space, particularly but not exclusively in the Jewish covenant. Then Jesus Christ came in the flesh for the sake of God's mission—preaching, serving, and witnessing to the reign of God.

The gospel of Jesus, then and now, is seen in "how his parables called his disciples to be forgiving, how his miracles called them to be agents of healing and wholeness, how his exorcisms called them to be opposed absolutely to evil in every form, how his inclusive lifestyle called them to be inclusive" (Bevans and Schroeder 2004, 358). All of these aspects are captured in Jesus' attitude and practice of table fellowship in a broad sense. Contrary to cultural-religious practices that understood holiness in terms of separation (the pure from the impure), Jesus witnessed to God's inclusive love and mercy, which flows over all boundaries. The healings and exorcisms of Jesus usually touched the lives of those considered impure; Jesus ate with sinners and tax-collectors; Jesus' total commitment to God's mission led to his death and resurrection; and Jesus' love and mission reached beyond the Jewish people. Jesus offered the hungry the true "bread of life" (Jn 6:35), so that "everyone who looks upon the Son and believes in him shall have eternal life" (Jn 6:40). Jesus came as a means of salvation for all peoples.

During a very down-to-earth and daily task of getting water, Jesus had a life-changing dialogue with the Samaritan woman. This encounter reminds us of how deeply God's word can touch, nourish, and challenge us in so many ways—practically, personally, spiritually, religiously. She was invited to share at the table of the "living water," which she immediately proceeded to share with others, even leaving her water jar behind.

Using images familiar to his listeners, Jesus' parables of the seeds and the weeds give us further hints of the mission of God. We have a responsibility to allow God's word to call us to conversion and to take root in our lives. While there is no shortage of challenges that sin tosses our way, we are assured that God's word has a power of its own to bear fruit. We are back to the bigger picture.

In the next chapter we will continue to follow the story of God's mission. The Spirit will lead those early Christian disciples in challenging and surprising ways.

Questions for Reflection

1. How does the explanation of table fellowship alter your understanding of the meaning of mission?
2. Share a story of your experience of the "new life" of God.
3. What "jar" do you need to leave behind in order to share God's message of love, compassion, and forgiveness with others?

Suggestions for Further Reading

Kirk, J. Andrew. *What Is Mission? Theological Explorations.* Minneapolis, MN: Fortress Press, 2000. Chapters 1–3. Further development of theological foundations of mission.

National Conference of Catholic Bishops. *To the Ends of the Earth: A Pastoral Statement on World Mission.* Washington, DC:

USCC, 1986. Paragraphs 22–50. Section 2, "Today's Mission-ary Task," from a major U.S. Catholic document on mission.

Senior, Donald, and Carroll Stuhlmueller. *The Biblical Founda-tions for Mission*. Maryknoll, NY: Orbis Books, 1983. Chapter 6, "Jesus and the Church's Mission"; Chapter 7, "The Mis-sion Theology of Paul." Classical treatment of Bible and mis-sion by two Catholic scholars.

3

The Spirit Leads the Disciples in New Directions

The Biblical Portrait of a Church Missionary by Nature

What happened to God's mission after Jesus' death and resurrection? Of the twelve apostles, Judas betrayed Jesus, Peter denied him, and it seems that John (with Jesus' mother, Mary) was the sole apostle at the cross. Joseph of Arimathaea, a member of the Jewish Sanhedrin, came forward to get permission to bury Jesus. A number of women—including Mary of Magdala, Mary the mother of James and Joseph, and the mother of Zebedee's sons—had faithfully accompanied Jesus from Galilee and stayed with him during his crucifixion (Mt 27:55–56). Several of these women were the first witnesses of Jesus' resurrection, and they ran immediately to tell the other disciples. The questioning of Thomas and the concerns of the two disciples on the road to Emmaus indicate that it took some time and much faith for the disciples to accept and understand the meaning of this astonishing news. However, it would require much more faith to accept and understand what would follow.

In this chapter we follow the steps of these early disciples of Jesus by walking through the Acts of the Apostles, that inspiring account of the Christian movement after Jesus' resurrection. We will see how this huddled handful of disciples moved out of the upper room at Pentecost and were led by God's Spirit to continue the mission of Jesus in very challenging and surprising ways. Initially, they remained within the Jewish world, but as events unfolded, they soon found themselves more and more engaged with Gentiles. This movement began with mission and eventually gave birth to the church. The Second Vatican Council reclaimed and reaffirmed this by stating, "The pilgrim Church is missionary by her very nature" (AG 2; see LG 1). In the words of the U.S. bishops, "To say 'church' is to say 'mission'" (TEE 16). The church exists not for itself but because of and for the sake of God's mission. Another way of saying this: *The church doesn't have a mission, but the mission has a church!*

Christianity shifts from being a small group within Judaism to being a new religion open to all peoples. These developments were crucial in forming and shaping the church and are essential for understanding mission today. This process unfolds in seven stages (see Bevans and Schroeder 2004, chap. 1) through the Acts of the Apostles, which Luke wrote as a second volume to his Gospel.

In order to get the full picture of the understanding of mission in the scriptures, one would have to study the entire New Testament. *The Biblical Foundations for Mission* by Donald Senior and the late Carroll Stuhlmueller is one of the best books to explore this topic in depth (see "Further Readings" at the end of this chapter). However, for our purposes in this book, we focus only on the Acts of the Apostles, because it provides the story that links Jesus' mission with the beginning of the church.

Before Pentecost (Acts 1): Disappointment and Expectation

Earlier we saw that the central message of Jesus' life and consequent death revolved around the reign of God. Contrary to popular understanding, most biblical and theological scholars believe that Jesus did not explicitly plan to found a church distinct from Judaism or to establish a full-blown mission to the Gentiles. Rather, Jesus was committed to heralding the imminent in-breaking of the reign of God, not to long-term planning. Some of his followers mistakenly understood this in political terms, as reflected in the words of the disciples at the ascension, "Lord, are you going to restore the rule to Israel now?" (Acts 1:6) "But despite the fact that both the establishment of a community separate from Israel and the idea of a mission beyond Israel were probably far from the thoughts of Jesus, one might still say that Jesus laid the foundation for both" (Bevans and Schroeder 2004, 14). The eventual understanding of mission and church were founded on the vision, person, and mission of Jesus. The establishment of the twelve apostles (symbolic of the twelve tribes of Israel), the appointment of Peter as leader, and the command to celebrate a meal in Jesus' memory provided that initial post-Easter community with a sense of identity and structure. Jesus' radical inclusive understanding of God was the spiritual foundation of his life and ministry, which was directed primarily toward the Jews but already had significant, though implicit, pointers beyond Israel. The full significance of this would evolve only with time and the guidance of the Spirit.

At this early stage the disciples returning to Jerusalem after the Ascension were most likely expecting the return of Jesus to initiate the imminent coming of God's reign on earth. They were told by Jesus that they would be baptized by the Spirit "within a few days" (1:5). After Jesus ascended, the "two men dressed in white" (1:10) told them, "This Jesus who has been taken from you will return, just as you saw him go up into the heavens" (1:11). So, since God's reign was about to break into history, the disciples replaced Judas through the election of Matthias (1:15–26) so that the number of the Twelve (who would judge the twelve tribes of Israel) was restored. Instead of going out to "Judea and Samaria, yes, even to the ends of the earth" (1:8), they stayed in Jerusalem. A sense of emptiness, awkwardness, and expectation hovered over them in these days of prayerful waiting.

Pentecost (Acts 2—5):
Receiving Power to Bear Witness

"When the day of Pentecost came" (Acts 2:1), the disciples experienced a fulfillment of Jesus' promise, but it was not what they expected. It was not the second coming of Jesus but an outpouring of the Spirit. It was not the end of time but a second chance for the Jews, through the disciples, to accept Jesus as the Messiah and so be saved "from this generation which has gone astray" (2:40). Many refer to Pentecost as the birthday of the church. While Pentecost is certainly a very key moment for the church, because the coming of the Spirit will lead the disciples in new directions in carrying out the mission of Christ and then in founding the church, the church is actually not fully born until the Jesus community sees itself as distinct from Judaism and crosses outside the boundaries of Judaism in mission. This does not occur in Jerusalem but later in Antioch (stage six).

People from many nations were gathered in Jerusalem at this time: "Parthians, Medes and Elamites; people from Mesopotamia, Judea and Cappadocia, Pontus and Asia, Phrygia and Pamphylia, Egypt, and the parts of Libya round Cyrene; as well as visitors from Rome—Jews and proselytes alike—Cretans and Arabs" (2:9–11). Some considered this wide representation of nations and references in Peter's speech to "all humankind" (2:17) and "all those still far off" (2:39) as the beginning of the church and the Gentile mission. However, *all of these people were Jewish*, by birth or conversion (2:11). Even though the Gentiles would enter God's reign after Israel responded positively to its "second chance," the disciples were addressing themselves to the Jewish people. An explicit mission to the Gentiles was still very far from their thoughts.

In fact, it seemed like the final days had arrived in Jerusalem. People were joining them daily (2:47; 5:14); they enjoyed an intense community life (2:42–47; 4:32–35); the apostles were working miracles and signs (2:43; 3:1–10); and even though they experienced some opposition from some Jewish religious leaders (4:1–7; 5:17–42), Christians were held in high esteem by many (5:12–16). The women and men of the Jesus movement saw themselves in continuity with and faithful to Jewish religious-cultural tradition. They continued to follow Jewish Law and to go to the Temple daily, and they felt no conflict with also following the teachings of the apostles, meeting in homes for the "breaking of bread" (2:42, 46), and proclaiming Jesus as "both Lord and Messiah" (2:36). But signs of change were on the horizon.

Stephen and the Hellenists (Acts 6—7):
Jewish Disciples Pushed beyond Their Comfort Zone

In chapters 6 and 7 of Acts this ideal picture of the community in Jerusalem is disturbed. The Greek-speaking disciples, called Hellenists, complained to the Hebrew-speaking disciples, called Hebrews, that the Hellenist widows were being overlooked in the daily distribution of food. The community met and appointed Stephen, Philip, and five others to attend to this need (Acts 6:1–6). These seven men had Greek names, and all of them were probably Hellenists. On the community level, this particular concern is addressed quite smoothly. However, the issue reflects an underlying linguistic, cultural and social diversity among the followers of Jesus in Jerusalem. What does this say about table fellowship? This situation also includes theological diversity, which will have other serious consequences. The Greek-speaking Jewish Christians or Hellenists were much more influenced by the broader Hellenistic world view. They held a less traditional view of Judaism, which allowed them, for example, to place the significance of Jesus over Moses. On the other hand, the Hebrew-speaking Jewish Christians in Jerusalem held a more traditional view of Judaism.

Stephen, one of the appointed seven, "was a man filled with grace and power, who worked great wonders and signs among the people" (6:8). He was apparently quite articulate and wise, since members of the Synagogue of Freedmen were not able to overcome him in debate (6:9). They then brought false charges against Stephen, and he was arrested and brought before the Sanhedrin (6:11–15). Stephen's speech (7:2–53) is very important, not for the movement toward the Gentiles, but for indicating the beginning of the shift away from traditional Judaism. Stephen outlines four crucial periods in Israel's history and how Israel consistently went against God's lead by opposing and killing God's representatives, the most recent being Jesus. From all that Stephen spoke, it was his profession of Jesus as the Just One (7:52) and Lord (7:59), in other words, as "the one means necessary for salvation" (Kilgallen 1989, 192), that led to his being stoned to death (7:58—8:2). Like Christ, Stephen forgave his persecutors. Cloaks were piled at the feet of Saul, who led the subsequent persecution against the followers of Jesus, particularly the Hellenists who, like Stephen, challenged the adequacy of Judaism.

Samaria and the Ethiopian Eunuch (Acts 8): To the Ends of the Earth?

Although the Hellenists were escaping the persecution in Jerusalem, that did not prevent them from preaching the good news. Philip, one of the other seven (Acts 6:5), was bold enough to preach even to the Samaritans. As we recall from Jesus' encounter with the Samaritan woman, the Samaritans, considered "half-Jews" both in terms of religion and race, were viewed as heretics and schismatics. Philip worked miracles and preached Jesus Christ to them (8:4–7). "Without exception, the crowds that heard Philip and saw the miracles he performed attended closely to what he had to say" (8:6). When the apostles, who had remained in Jerusalem, heard about this reception, they sent Peter and John to check it out (8:14). They not only approved what was happening and laid hands on the newly baptized Samaritans so they could likewise receive the Holy Spirit, but Peter and John even preached in other Samaritan towns as they returned to Jerusalem (8:15–17, 25). They were taking Jesus' initial encounter with the Samaritans much further.

This is followed by the wonderful story of the conversion of the Ethiopian eunuch. The initiative of God's mission is very explicit in this account: an angel tells Philip to go to the road (8:26); the Spirit tells him to run up to the eunuch's chariot (8:29); and the Spirit sweeps Philip away after the baptism (8:39). While it is not clear whether the Ethiopian was a Gentile, a convert to Judaism, and/or a eunuch, physically speaking, he was a person who was very close to Judaism (if he wasn't a Jew) returning from a pilgrimage to Jerusalem and reading the prophet Isaiah (8:27–28). He was the chief treasurer of the queen of Ethiopia, which was the last known geographical region to the south.

Now to the encounter itself. When Philip reached the chariot, he heard the eunuch reading the prophet Isaiah and asked him whether he understood it (8:30). "How can I," the man replied, "unless someone explains it to me?" (8:31). Philip then climbed on the chariot and, beginning with that particular scripture (Is 53:7–8), proceeded to explain the good news of Jesus to him (Acts 8:35). "When they come to some water, the eunuch asks if anything prevents him from being baptized; and since nothing does—not his physical state, not his foreignness, not his blackness, not his being a Gentile—Philip baptizes him (8:38)" (Bevans and Schroeder 2004, 22). Philip was swept away immediately to continue preaching "in all the towns until he reached Caesarea" (8:40) and the eunuch "went on his way rejoicing" (8:39) to Ethiopia, the "ends of the earth" (1:8). The circle of believers continues to widen.

Cornelius and His Household (Acts 10:1—11:18): Peter and the Gentile Mission

The dramatic conversion of Saul from persecutor of the followers of Jesus to the key promoter of Jesus as the Messiah ("Christ," the "Anointed One") appears three times in Acts (9:1–19; 22:5–16; 26:10–18). Falling on the ground and blinded, Saul three days later, with the assistance of Ananias, would regain his sight, be baptized, and spend the rest of his life proclaiming Jesus as the Son of God. We shall return to the significant role of Saul, later named Paul, in the seventh stage of our treatment of Acts.

At this point we shall carefully and reflectively examine the conversion of the Gentile Cornelius and his household. This moment has been considered by some as "the most critical phase of the expansion of God's people" (Johnson 1992, 186). While it is not clear whether the Ethiopian eunuch was a Gentile, there is no doubt that the Roman centurion Cornelius living in Caesarea was. He and his whole household were devout and God-fearing, and "he was in the habit of giving generously to the people and constantly prayed to God" (10:2).

Table fellowship, which was such an important element of Jesus' mission of announcing the reign of God, becomes the central issue in this encounter between Peter and Cornelius. This simple story indicates a turning point for Christianity. The underlying question was whether Jewish Christians could share a common meal (and therefore eventually the Eucharist) with Gentile Christians. This was the challenge facing the Christian communities to whom Luke was writing in Acts. The deeper realization was that the God of the Jewish people, as revealed in Jesus Christ, was the God calling all nations to one table.

The scene opens with Cornelius in prayer, receiving a vision to send for a man named Peter in Joppa (10:3–6). While Cornelius's messengers are on their way, God's Spirit is also at work within Peter. During prayer, Peter has a vision of something like a big sheet being let down from heaven and filled with all kinds of animals and birds (10:9–12). A voice then instructs Peter to kill and eat what is before him. However, holding in mind the traditional Jewish dietary restrictions, he responds, "Sir, it is unthinkable! I have never yet eaten anything unclean or impure in my life" (10:14). And then Peter is confronted by an astonishing response: "What God has purified you are not to call unclean" (10:15).

This sequence happened three times, and Peter remained puzzled by its meaning. Then the three messengers of Cornelius arrive, and Peter is instructed by the Spirit to go with them: "Go downstairs and set out with them unhesitatingly; it is I who sent them"(10:20). Peter received the messengers, *Gentiles*, as guests for the evening (10:23). Nothing is said about sharing food, but staying under one roof was already an indication of new things to come.

The next day Peter set out for Caesarea and entered Cornelius's home, which was crowded with "his relatives and close friends" (10:24). Peter realized that "it is not proper for a Jew to associate with a Gentile," but he also knew that "God has made it clear . . . that no one should call anyone unclean or impure" (10:28). Cornelius explained his vision and then asked Peter to speak to them "whatever directives the Lord has given you" (10:33). While this story is commonly known as the conversion of Cornelius, it is likewise the conversion of Peter! Having been confused and challenged by his earlier vision, Peter now experiences a dramatic reversal in this cultural-religious world. "The truth I have now come to realize is that God does not have favorites, but that anybody of any nationality who fears God and does what is right is acceptable to him" (10:34–35).

Peter then proceeded to share the good news of Jesus Christ, who is Lord of all (10:36). In the middle of his preaching, the Spirit came down upon all of those gathered, to the utter surprise of the Jewish believers who had accompanied Peter from Joppa (10:44–45). "Peter himself then said, 'Could anyone refuse the water of baptism to these people, now they have received the Holy Spirit just as much as we have?'" (10:47).

After their baptism, they begged Peter to stay with them for some days and, in light of later accusations, he ate with them as well.

When Peter eventually returned to Jerusalem, he had some explaining to do. Many criticized him for baptizing the Gentiles, but the pressing concern seems to have been Peter's table fellowship: "So you have been visiting the uncircumcised and eating with them, have you?" (11:3). On this first level of daily life, this incident immediately confronts the social and religious principles of their traditional way of living and seeing the world. Second, Peter's table fellowship is a symbol and concrete sign of the universal scope of God's mission. "Samaritans were one thing; they were, after all, half-Jews. The Ethiopian eunuch was probably considered a rare exception. But here was a whole Gentile household receiving admittance into the community" (Bevans and Schroeder 2004, 24–25). Peter then recounted what had happened (Acts 11:4–17). When he came to the part of their baptism, Peter said, "Who was I to stand in God's way?" (11:17). In the end, the Jerusalem community was satisfied with this surprising and challenging development, as they realized that even the Gentiles could receive "life-giving repentance" (11:19). As we will see below, these issues will be addressed again more formally at the Council of Jerusalem (15:4–29), but the evolving shape of mission has received initial acceptance and affirmation.

What an amazing story of God's Spirit leading the early disciples in such new and unexpected ways. How challenging and revolutionary! The world view of Peter and the Jerusalem community was challenged by Jesus' gospel. At the same time, how wonderful and life-giving! The good news demanded repentance and promised new life for the Samaritans, the Ethiopian eunuch, and now Cornelius's household. And the circle of believers continues to widen.

Antioch (Acts 11:19–29):
Mission Matures

Luke's narrative builds upon and moves beyond the Cornelius story to its climax. The next episode, or stage, lasts only twenty-one verses, but perhaps it is even more important. The eminent Scottish missiologist Andrew Walls considers this incident at Antioch "one of the most critical events in Christian history" (Walls 1996, 52). We shift from Peter and the community in Jerusalem back to the Greek-speaking followers of Jesus, who, like Philip, had escaped the persecutions. These Hellenists "usually proclaimed the message only to Jews" but "some of them . . . went to Antioch where they started preaching to the Gentiles" (Acts 11:19–20). And "a great number believed and were converted to the Lord" (11:21). Rather than the isolated event with the single household of Cornelius, we find an explicit and intentional mission to the Gentiles, and Jewish and Gentile converts living side by side. This takes place in Antioch, the fourth largest city in the Roman Empire.

Several elements point to the radical nature of this turn of events. First of all, the Greek-speaking disciples used a new term, "lord Jesus" (11:20), when they preached to the Gentiles in Antioch. Rather than using the Jewish title *messiah (Christos)*, which was a rather foreign term to the Greek mind, they used *lord (Kyrios)*, which the Gentiles could understand better from their religious and cultural background. This was a radical move because "for the first time, the gospel message was being presented in terms that moved beyond the pale of Judaism" (Bevans and Schroeder 2004, 26). It also was essential, since it is doubtful whether the Gentiles "could have understood the significance of Jesus in any other way" (Walls 1996, 35). This is the first of many instances of the gospel being translated and presented in terms and images that make sense in the languages and cultures of those hearing it.

A second sign of the importance of this moment was that the community of Jerusalem sent Barnabas, a highly regarded disciple who was himself a Hellenist, to see what was happening in Antioch. He recognized that this was the work of God and, in the spirit of his name, which means "son of encouragement" (Acts 4:36), he "encouraged them all to remain faithful to the Lord with heartfelt devotion" (11:23). Barnabas did not have to "complete" the evangelizing process, as Peter and John had to do with the Samaritans earlier (8:15–17). Furthermore, Barnabas went to Tarsus to find Saul and bring him to Antioch, where the two of them worked together for a year (11:25–26). This was important both for Antioch and the eventual spread of the gospel to many other places.

The third indication that the Jesus movement was seeing itself as church is that "it was at Antioch that the disciples were first called 'Christians'" (11:26). Even though this name may have been given by others with a somewhat derogatory meaning, it does indicate that the Jesus movement was being identified and identifying itself as a group on its own, not as a subgroup of Judaism. It is possible that the word *church* was also used for the first time at Antioch (see Bevans and Schroeder 2004, 27).

There was quite a shift from the pre-Pentecost perspective and experience to Antioch. Stephen's speech had hinted at this difference between the Jesus movement and Judaism. The developments after Stephen's death make this clearer. As more and more Jews (but not all) reject the gospel and more and more Gentiles accept it, the Spirit leads Christians on a more long-term and ever-expanding mission than these early followers could have imagined. "With expanding consciousness of mission comes an expanding consciousness of being church" (Bevans and Schroeder 2004, 27). Antioch marks the church's real "birthday."

Universal Mission (Acts 12—28): Missional and Church Self-Consciousness Spreads

The first six stages in birthing the church reached the climax in chapter 11; now the final stage, the remaining seventeen chapters of Acts, represents the early years of development and challenge. The accounts in Acts 12:1–11 of the execution of James (brother of John and one of the Twelve) and Peter's arrest and escape from prison signal the shift away from the Jerusalem community. Chapter 13 and the rest of Acts focus on Paul's mission.

Under the Spirit's guidance the community at Antioch sent Barnabas and Saul on what would later be called Paul's first missionary journey (Acts 12:25—13:3). Luke shifts to Saul's Roman name, Paul (13:9), and the lead in mission begins to shift from Barnabas to Paul. Traveling by sea and land, they eventually arrived in the Roman colony of Pisidian Antioch in Asia Minor. Paul began by preaching in the synagogue to the Jews and some Gentile God-fearers (who were drawn to Judaism to various degrees but stopped short of circumcision in joining the Jewish faith). At first, many of the Jews were very interested in what they heard from Paul. However, on the following Sabbath, when "almost the whole town [which would have included many more Gentiles] assembled to hear the word of God" (13:44), the Jews turned against Paul's message. Paul and Barnabas responded with the first of three formal statements in this second half of Acts (13:46–47; 18:4–7; 28:25–28)—although the gospel must first be preached to the Jews, since they have rejected it, "we must turn to the Gentiles" (13:46). The Gentiles were "very happy to hear this and they thanked the Lord for the word of God" (13:48). "Thus the word of the Lord spread through the whole countryside" (13:39). Paul continued to preach to the Jews, but a pattern had been set. After further hardships and successes, Paul and Barnabas eventually returned to Antioch to report that God "had opened the door of faith to the Gentiles" (14:27).

While this is received as good news by many, others in the Jerusalem community, especially some Pharisees who have become Christians, feared the consequences of this development. They believed that Gentile Christians needed to follow Jewish customs, including circumcision, if there were to be any realistic possibility of Jews and Gentiles forming a common Christian community. Some of them caused confusion and dissension when they began teaching this in Antioch, and so "it was decided that Paul, Barnabas, and some others should go up to see the apostles and presbyters in Jerusalem about this question" (15:2–3). We now approach what has become known as the Council of Jerusalem (around the year 49). This gathering would be the watershed moment for dealing formally with the fundamental issues underlying the recent succession of events, particularly regarding Cornelius's household, the community in Antioch, and the first missionary journey of Paul and Barnabas. In other words, this meeting in Jerusalem was the official discussion, by a number of the key leaders of the young Christian church, of what had been happening "on the ground" in their Spirit-led community.

After much discussion of whether Gentile Christians needed to be circumcised and to follow the Mosaic Law (implicitly including the issue of table fellowship), Peter reminded the assembly that God had approved what had happened among the Gentiles "by granting the Holy Spirit to them just as he did to us" (15:8). After Peter's speech, "the whole assembly fell silent," and Paul and Barnabas then recounted "all the signs and wonders God had worked among the Gentiles" (15:12). James, the leader of the Jerusalem community, affirmed that, since God was "taking from among the Gentiles, a people to bear his name . . . we ought not to cause God's Gentile converts any difficulties" (15:14, 19). This act of faith in discerning God's Spirit at work in unforeseen and challenging ways was the "mark of approval" on the future direction and "face" of the church.

In a 1979 article Karl Rahner, one of the most important Catholic theologians since the mid-1960s, compared the Council of Jerusalem with the Second Vatican Council. At that first council the church recognized that Christianity is not restricted to Jewish culture but rather is inclusive of Jews and Gentiles. Over the course of church history, however, Christianity became equated with Western cultures. Becoming a Christian implied taking on Western customs. For example, some missionaries in Papua New Guinea linked the custom of women wearing blouses with being a proper Catholic. However, Rahner points to the fact that, similar to the Council of Jerusalem, the Second Vatican Council acknowledges again and reaffirms that being a Christian is not limited to any cultural way but rather is open to being received and expressed by the vast array of cultures in the world.

From the end of chapter 15 of Acts until Paul's arrest in chapter 21, we hear of Paul's mission journeys in Europe and Asia, preaching to both Jews and Gentiles. However, Jewish opposition grows, and there is a decisive turn to the Gentiles. The remaining chapters of Acts recount Paul's arrest and difficulties in

Jerusalem and later in Caesarea and his journey to and stay in Rome. In Rome, the Jews reject Paul's preaching and he concludes that "this salvation of God has been transmitted to the Gentiles—who heed it" (28:28). Acts concludes with these two verses: "For two full years Paul stayed on in his rented lodgings, *welcoming all who came to him. With full assurance*, and without any hindrance whatever, *he preached the reign of God and taught about the Lord Jesus Christ*" (28:30–31, emphasis added). What a shift from the beginning to the end of Acts! And yet, there is a direct line from God's mission, to Jesus' mission, to the church's mission.

A Tiny Church with a Universal Mission

We have seen how the mission of God for us and our world took shape in quite a dramatic way. It was old—a continuation and manifestation of that mission of God that has been present from the beginning of creation and humanity, and of that same mission of the Spirit and of the Word, Jesus Christ. But it was also something new. The Spirit was leading that small group of disciples to continue God's mission in new and surprising ways. The disciples now constituted a tiny *ekklesia* ("assembly," the root of our word *church*) with a growing consciousness that its message that Jesus was the savior of the world was destined for all of humanity. The universal mission of God, in other words, now had a church.

Remember Peter's account of the household of Cornelius receiving the same Spirit that he and other disciples had received at Pentecost (11:15)? "Equality of gift (the Holy Spirit) means equality of salvation, which implies equality among all believers, whether circumcised or uncircumcised, Jews or Gentiles. This equality necessarily includes table fellowship, for that is the heart of Christian unity and fellowship" (Nguyen 2004, 105). The breaking of the bread among Jewish and Gentile Christians was the down-to-earth realization of the challenge and the blessing that God was presenting to the community of the Acts of the Apostles and other early Christian communities. The same Spirit was calling both Gentile and Jewish Christians to repent, to embrace the reign of

God, to enter into one community, and to witness to Christ as the Savior of all peoples. In this way we can say that the church was born, not so much on Pentecost, but rather in places like Antioch, where the Jewish Christians saw themselves as distinct from, but not in contradiction with, their Jewish tradition and faith. A new reality and a new community, called church, came into being.

The church was born out of the loving and redeeming flow of God's universal mission. Walking through the Acts of the Apostles provides an excellent narrative behind the rediscovery of the Second Vatican Council, which was our starting point for this chapter: "The pilgrim Church is missionary by her very nature" (AG 2). To repeat, the church doesn't have a mission, but the mission has a church.

This realization was not only for the church as a whole, as fragile as it was at that point, but it also touched the core of individuals who were beginning to be called Christians. They began to understand and live out the inseparable connection among baptism, mission, and church. Thus we can say that baptism is also missionary by nature. This dynamic will become much clearer as we continue with the story of mission in the next chapter.

Questions for Reflection

1. What was the most interesting new idea that struck you from our survey of the Acts of the Apostles?
2. Can you describe an incident, similar to the Peter and Cornelius story, in which your or your church's horizons were widened unexpectedly?
3. Describe the connection between mission and church with an image or in your own words.

Suggestions for Further Reading

Bevans, Stephen B., and Roger P. Schroeder. *Constants in Context: A Theology of Mission for Today.* Maryknoll, NY: Orbis Books, 2004. Chapter 1. More detailed treatment of the development of mission and church in the Acts of the Apostles.

Esler, Philip Francis. *Community and Gospel in Luke–Acts: The Social and Political Motivations of Lucan Theology.* Cambridge, UK: Cambridge University Press, 1987. Scholarly study of the social and political issues in the Acts of the Apostles.

Johnson, Luke Timothy. *The Acts of the Apostles.* Sacra Pagina 5. Collegeville, MN: The Liturgical Press, 1992. Scholarly biblical commentary on the Acts of the Apostles.

Rahner, Karl. "Toward a Fundamental Theological Interpretation of Vatican II." *Theological Studies* 40 (1979), 716–27. Important theological article drawing a comparison between the Council of Jerusalem and the Second Vatican Council.

Senior, Donald, and Carroll Stuhlmueller. *The Biblical Foundations for Mission.* Maryknoll, NY: Orbis Books, 1983. Chapter 7, "The Mission Theology of Paul; Chapter 11, "The Mission Perspective of Luke-Acts"; Chapter 12, "The Johannine Theology of Mission"; Chapter 14, "Conclusion: The Biblical Foundations for Mission." Classical treatment of Bible and mission by two Catholic authors.

Wright, N. T. *Paul in Fresh Perspective.* Minneapolis: Fortress Press, 2005. A fresh look at how Paul interprets the message of Jesus for the Greek-speaking world, being both faithful to the vision of the expected Messiah in the Hebrew scriptures and also expanding it with a full recognition of the unique and universal significance of Jesus as the Christ.

4

Mission from the Early Church to the Fall of Constantinople (100–1453)

• •

House Churches, Monks,
Mendicants, and Beguines

In the last chapter we reviewed the inspiring divine-human story of mission by the first generation of Christ's disciples. How did Christians moved by the same Spirit of the prophets, Jesus, and the Acts of the Apostles continue to live out their baptismal identity in mission? How will the newborn church grow, change, and struggle as the community of Jesus that is to be missionary by nature? We might be tempted to immediately fast-forward to our present day. However, it is important to see how the understanding and actual practice of mission developed over time. Just as we are inspired by and learn something important for our faith today from the Acts of the Apostles, there are many inspirations and lessons waiting for us throughout the history of mission.

In Chapter 7 we will study the six components of contemporary mission, that is, the various forms that mission can take depending on different situations in today's world. These components are witness and proclamation; liturgy, prayer, and contemplation; justice, peace, and the integrity of creation; interreligious and secular dialogue; inculturation; and reconciliation. In our glimpse into the past we will find models and representatives of these various ways of doing mission.

We will see the human side of the church with its limitations, prejudices, and sinfulness. We will also see the divine side with its faithfulness, courage, and grace. Both aspects need to be taken together to see the truth. Christian history has not been uniform but rather one of great diversity and even contradiction at times. Christianity has not been the monopoly of one geographical part of the world. Many people have the impression that Christianity always was and still is a Western religion. That wasn't true at the beginning, and it isn't true now. Furthermore, to fill the gaps in traditional Christian history we include the roles of women, laity, and non-Western persons within the whole picture in mission. With all of this in mind, we hope to understand and appreciate more fully, but never completely, how Christian men and women have tried to participate in God's mission over time and through space. The church continues to face the challenge of being always faithful while ever changing.

Covering the whole story of Christian mission is too much for us to attempt here. We will divide the history into six chronological periods that were fairly distinct moments of Christian mission. After a brief overview of each time period, we will take a couple glimpses of mission in action and then reflect on how these are relevant for us today. Rather than trying to view the entire film covering two thousand years, we will be content with looking at snapshots. Another way of imagining this is that we are going back in a time capsule and just dropping in at various moments to catch Christians in the act of mission.

This chapter explores the first three periods, beginning around the year 100 and concluding with the fall of Constantinople (present-day Istanbul) in 1453 to Muslim rule, marking the end of the eleven-hundred-year history of Byzantine Christianity. (For a more detailed treatment of these three time periods, see Bevans and Schroeder 2004, chaps. 3–5.)

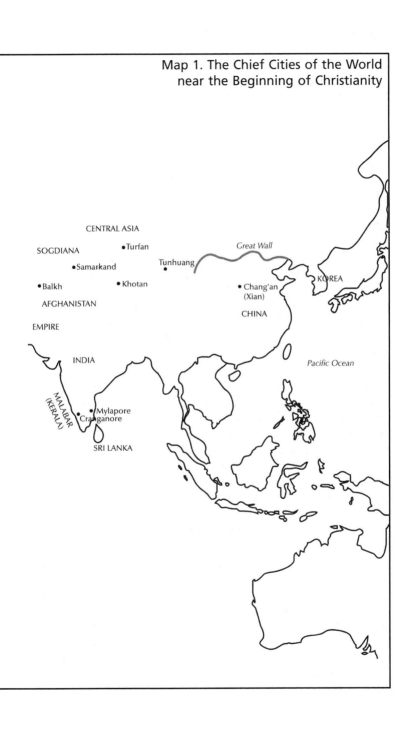

Map 1. The Chief Cities of the World near the Beginning of Christianity

Mission in the Early Church (100–301):
Individual Christians in a Variety of Situations

How did the church develop after the events associated with the household of Cornelius, the city of Antioch, the Council of Jerusalem, and the ministry of Paul? While we usually think of Christianity moving west toward Rome, the Christian faith also spread equally to the north to present-day Armenia; to the east across Iraq (Mesopotamia), Iran (Persia), as far as India; and to the south to Egypt, Ethiopia, and across northern Africa (see Map 1). For example, the Mesopotamian city of Edessa (in southern Turkey), which was strategically situated at the crossroads of two major ancient trade routes, was a key center for Syriac-speaking Christians and the site of an early Christian council and the oldest known church building (before the year 200). An amazing story of this period occurred on the southwest Malabar Coast of India, where a small merchant community of Christians, who traced its apostolic roots to the apostle Thomas, developed; they are known today as Saint Thomas Christians. This first period ends in the year 301 with the semi-independent kingdom of Armenia (which was much larger than the current country of Armenia) becoming the first nation officially to declare itself Christian—some years before the Roman Empire did so.

The second and third centuries of Christianity have received much attention in recent years. For example, the Second Vatican Council looked back to its roots in the life and theology of the early church by reclaiming the missionary nature of the church.

Christians: At Home and in the Marketplace

In the early years of the church Christians outside the Roman Empire—that is, in present-day Armenia, Iraq, Iran and India—lived their newfound faith openly and freely. However, those who lived under the rule of Rome, which enveloped the Mediterranean Sea, had a more difficult time during this period. They couldn't build churches or gather in public. They were accused of being cannibals (for eating the body of Christ) and traitors (for refusing to worship the emperor). Men and women died for their faith during the occasional periods of public persecution.

The home was the center of Christian life. Certain houses, especially larger ones, were designated for the weekly gatherings for prayer, bible study, community discussion, sharing resources, and the breaking of the bread. They are known as house churches. Some went through major renovation in order to accommodate the growing numbers of Christians. During the week the home was the place for many informal conversations about the Christian faith with friends and neighbors.

The present-day Church of SS. Giovanni e Paolo near the Coliseum in Rome was built over the site of a house church that is now open to the public. Entering on the side of the hill some three stories below the current church, one walks into a home with well-preserved Roman paintings on the wall. Winding up and around to the next level, one finds a three-foot "shelf" that was most likely used for the Eucharist. The remains of two deceased members of the home, Giovanni and Paolo, who were martyred for their faith in the fourth century, are on the other side of the wall. Their painted images, as well as those of three others who were subsequently martyred, adorn the walls of this space that was set aside both to remember those who died for their faith and to strengthen those who strove to live out their faith.

Early Christians also witnessed to their faith outside the home. Most lived in crowded urban areas, where probably as many as half the children died at birth or as infants, and where fires, earthquakes, and epidemics devastated the lives of thousands. Christians took care of orphans and widows, extending their care for the needy and sick to non-Christians. This action did not go unnoticed by others and marked the beginning of simple hospitals. We also have written reports of Christians having informal conversations in the marketplaces, laundries, and shops. One modern writer, Michael Green, calls this "gossiping the gospel":

> This must often have been not formal preaching, but the informal chattering to friends and chance acquaintances, in homes and wine shops, on walks, and around market stalls. They went everywhere gossiping the gospel; they did it naturally, enthusiastically, and with the conviction of those who are not paid to say that sort of thing. Consequently, they were taken seriously, and the movement spread. (Green 1970, 173)

Beyond their local surroundings, there are indications that Christians also brought their faith with them when they traveled as merchants, artisans, emigrants, soldiers, and slaves. Christianity spread rapidly through "ordinary" baptized Christians who witnessed to their faith in the face of opposition, sometimes to the point of death, but most through their daily living. And it started in the home.

Women: Witnesses at the Heart of Mission

Another snapshot from the early church is a picture of women in mission. We already saw the inclusiveness of women in Jesus' ministry, particularly in the incident with the Samaritan woman. Christianity continued to be particularly appealing to women. In contrast to broader society, the high regard in which the Christian community held the human dignity of women was reflected, for example, in its stance against abortion, infanticide (most often girls), divorce, incest, adultery, and polygamy. All were treated equally as children of God. "Not only Gentiles and slaves but also women could be full and equal members of this community" (Ruether and McLaughlin 1979, 32).

Women's role in mission began in the home. First of all, since women were the majority of Christians and there were not as many eligible Christian men for husbands, they often married non-Christians. There are written accounts of such women leading their husbands and the extended household—which often included servants, tenants, and business partners—to faith in Christ. Second, women were influential in the many Christian gatherings in the home. In the New Testament we read of women leading house churches—such as Prisca (Rom 16:5; 1 Cor 16:19), Nympha (Col 4:15), and possibly Phoebe (Rom 16:17), Chloe (1 Cor 1:11), Lydia (Acts 16:14–15, 40), and Martha (Lk 10:38). We can assume that this tradition continued into the second and third centuries. Third, women also shared ("gossiped") the gospel when gathered outside the home. Celsus, who criticized Christians, wrote of women talking about their faith in the laundry and the marketplace.

Women were also martyred. One of the very powerful writings of the early church is "The Passion of Sts. Perpetua and Felicity."

This was so popular that Saint Augustine years later was worried that it was more widely read in North Africa than the gospels. Perpetua was a fairly wealthy married woman with a newborn son living in Carthage (see Map 1). This African woman had gone against the law prohibiting conversion and baptism. Perpetua refused to deny her Christian faith, despite prison, separation from her nursing child, and appeals from her elderly father. Her servant Felicity, who was pregnant, was arrested with her. The two women, formerly mistress and servant and now sisters in Christ, died together in the amphitheater because of their Christian faith in the year 203. Blandina, a slave girl and recent convert, was martyred for her faith in Vienne (southern France) in 177. An eyewitness account of her martyrdom points out the strong connection between the death of Christ and that of a martyr. The suffering and death of martyrs was a source of inspiration for their fellow Christians and a witness that drew others to the faith.

> And because she [Blandina] appeared as if hanging on a cross, and because of her earnest prayers, she inspired the combatants with great zeal. For they . . . beheld with their outward eyes, in the form of their sister, him who was crucified for them, that he might persuade those who believe on him, that every one who suffers for the glory of Christ has fellowship always with the living God. (Eusebius V, 1 [41])

In terms of women in more "official" ministry, Paul in the New Testament (Reid 1997; Smith 2007) referred to women as co-workers—Phoebe (Rom 16:1–2) and Junia (Rom 16:7) as traveling missionaries, and the four prophesying daughters of Philip (Acts 21:9). We have later evidence of the preaching and leadership of Maximilla and Thecla in Asia Minor. However, by the end of the third century the official roles for women disappeared, with the exception of deaconesses in the East. This decline in official ministries should not detract from the primary contribution of women to the overall picture of mission in this early period of the church.

By the year 301, Armenia and Syria outside the Roman Empire were strong Christian centers from which the gospel continued to spread across Asia. In the Roman Empire about half the people in Asia Minor (roughly modern-day Turkey) and many in Egypt and North Africa had become Christians, while there were very few in the northernmost sections of the empire and in rural areas in general. Within the entire Roman Empire, Christians had grown at the astonishing rate of 40 percent a decade (Stark 1996, 6), so that they were over 10 percent of the total population around 300.

What can we learn from the early church? Ordinary baptized Christians were the primary agents of mission. Both women and men had no doubt that their baptism made them full members of the church and responsible to share the good news of Christ, with or without words. The martyr was the ideal Christian, one who committed his or her life totally to Christ. Those interested in becoming Christians were to be transformed into persons with such faith, motivation, and identity through an intensive catechumenate process. It is no coincidence that this program was reinstated as the RCIA (Rite of Christian Initiation of Adults) when the Second Vatican Council reclaimed the missionary nature of the church, baptism, and Eucharist. Every baptized person is necessarily called to share in God's mission within her/his own situation as in the early church.

In a Chicago parish a dozen young adults were preparing for baptism or full communion in the Catholic Church through an RCIA program. One evening they were reflecting on the theme of mission. Since they didn't see themselves standing on a soapbox preaching on a street corner, they didn't see themselves as doing mission. The presenter for the evening asked them to pinpoint the impetus for their decision to enter the church. Each one named a person—a spouse, a co-worker, a neighbor, an acquaintance. The presenter said, "We should go and do the same."

The early Christians witnessed to their faith through simple actions and words in their daily life, whether at home or in the marketplace. How inspiring and challenging their witness and proclamation continue to be for us! Some Christians are instruments of God's mission in their neighborhood, while others need passports to follow their missionary call.

The house church provides a wonderful image of table fellowship and mission. The place where they ate, slept, showed hospitality, and lived their faith on a daily basis was also the place where they talked with others about the gospel and celebrated the Eucharist. And this table fellowship in the broader sense—expanding the table to include God's extended family—was demonstrated by their practice of informally "gossiping the gospel," quietly witnessing their Christian faith, and providing health care in the neighborhood.

Mission and the Monastic Movement (313–907): From Constantine to the Fall of the T'ang Dynasty

Around the year 313, Emperor Constantine started a process that signaled a new phase for the church and mission. First, the status of Christianity in the Roman Empire began to shift from a religion which was tolerated at best and persecuted at worst to the officially endorsed religion of the empire. Second, Constantine shifted the capital from Rome to Byzantium and renamed it Constantinople. That city became the political-religious center of the Byzantine Church (eventually called the Orthodox Church) for the next eleven hundred years. The third consequence was that the Persian Empire began to persecute tens of thousands of Christians within its domain, since Christianity had now become the accepted religion of its longtime enemy. Another world event, the beginning of Islam in the seventh century, has a tremendous impact on all these Christian peoples. Muslim Arab rule was established over almost half of the Christian world within about a hundred years of the prophet Muhammad's death.

During this six-hundred-year period a variety of monastic movements emerged around the world and became the primary means of mission. Thousands of people seeking a way to live a more intentional and ascetic Christian life went to the deserts of Egypt and the wildernesses of Syria. Communities of monks and nuns developed, and the idea spread to Palestine, Ethiopia, Asia Minor, Italy, Gaul (France), Ireland, England, and Persia. The long list of those associated with these movements include Benedict and Scholastica, Boniface and Lioba, Martin of Tours, Melania the Younger, Patrick of Ireland, Brigid of Kildare, Augustine of Canterbury, and Hilda of Whitby. The monastic movement of the Syriac-speaking Christians spread across the Persian Empire and central Asia all the way to China. The year 907 marks the end of the first period of Christianity in China and the decline of monasticism's leading role in Christian mission in general.

East Syrian Monks: Traveling the Silk Road to China

In the overview of the early church above, we noted the ancient Syriac-speaking Christian tradition represented by Edessa and peoples of present-day Iraq and Iran. One of those who signed the Nicene Creed in 325 identified himself as "John the Persian, of the churches of the whole of Persia and in the great India" (Moffett 1992, 101). This Persian or East Syrian Church was later labeled by others as Nestorian, because its Syriac theological formulation of the nature and person of Jesus was not accepted by the broader church. This complex theological difference notwithstanding, tens of thousands of these Christians were martyred for their faith in the Persian Empire, and, despite the hardships under the Persian and later the Muslim rules, they carried the faith across Asia. The East Syrian monasteries were very important for preserving Christian identity and for theological, spiritual, and medical training. Furthermore, this network of monasteries, which stretched from Persia to India by the middle of the fourth century, provided centers for mission and refuge for Christian travelers across Asia and into China.

In 635, a small band of East Syrian monks led by Alopen traveled along the Silk Road and arrived in Chang'an (present-day Xian), the capital of the great Chinese Empire and the largest city of the world at that time (see Map 1). Fortunately, the T'ang dynasty then ruling China was open to other religions. The emperor asked the monks to bring him a Chinese translation of some Christian writings. Alopen and others spent three years preparing these translations. The emperor was so impressed that he granted them permission to preach the gospel with these words: "The [Christian] message is lucid and clear; the teachings will benefit all; and they should be practiced throughout the land." The emperor even financed the building of the first Chinese church in 638. The construction of other churches and monasteries soon followed. At the same time, Christians needed to learn how to live peacefully with the followers of other religions.

A nine-foot-tall stone tablet recording the story of Alopen, the emperor's decree, and the early history of the church in China was erected in 781 at a Christian monastery in the village of Lou Guan Tai, about sixty miles from Chang'an. This stone testament can be found today in a museum in the ancient city of Xian. At the original site of the monument in Lou Guan Tai there is a very large temple and garden of the Taoist religion at the base of the hill and a small Buddhist community next to the foundation of the ancient Christian monastery. This current setting reflects the interreligious world in which those East Syrian monk-missionaries and the first generations of Chinese Christians lived. They were challenged to witness faithfully to and proclaim their faith while living peacefully with the neighboring Buddhists and Taoists. Thirteen hundred years later, Catholic communities in the region of Lou Guan Tai acknowledge their early Christian roots.

Copies of the first Chinese Christian writings (sutras) of Alopen and others were discovered in 1907 in western China in a cave, where they had been hidden for protection for almost a thousand years. These writings demonstrate how Christians described God to the Chinese and people of other faiths.

> Nobody has the ability to see God. Truly, God is like the wind. Who can see the wind? God is not still but moves on the earth at all times. He is in everything and everywhere. Humanity lives only because it is filled with God's life-giving breath. Peace comes only when you can rest secure in your own place, when your heart and mind rest in God. . . . All great teachers such as the Buddhas are moved by this wind and there is nowhere in the world where this Wind does not reach and move. (Palmer 2001, 159–60)

The early moment of openness to the East Syrian monks and Christianity began to close with changing political winds of suspicion toward the influence of outsiders. An imperial decree in 845 significantly reduced the total number of monasteries in China, and many monks and priests were compelled to enter secular life. The final blow to this first period of Christianity came with the end of the tolerant T'ang dynasty in 907.

Cyril and Methodius: Apostles to the Slavs

We step back to the beginning of this time period to recall that one of the decisions of Constantine around the year 313 was to shift the capital of the empire from Rome to Constantinople. Rome and the West Roman Empire soon declined due to invasions by Germanic tribes and internal corruption. However, the East Roman Empire, with Constantinople as its capital, thrived and became the Byzantine Empire. It brought the church and state together in the attempt to be a Christian people. The church was known first as the Byzantine Church and later as the Orthodox Church. The Holy Roman Empire developed later within the territory that had been the West Roman Empire. At the time of this next snapshot from the history of mission, the Byzantine/Orthodox Church and the church of the Holy Roman Empire were both in union with the pope in Rome. Yet there was tremendous tension between them.

The particular monastic tradition that developed in the Byzantine Church reflected the close link between the church and state. While mission in this context sometimes was violent, there also were outstanding gentle approaches. The most famous is the work of missionary-monks Cyril and Methodius, who were named co-patrons of Europe by Pope John Paul II in 1980.

The two brothers, Cyril and Methodius, were born in the early ninth century in Greece. The position of their father in imperial administration opened doors for them in politics. However, both were likewise drawn to the monastic life of contemplation and study. The brothers were called from the monastery to be a part of official cultural and diplomatic trips among the Slavic peoples. So, when the prince of Moravia (a Central European state) requested Christian missionaries from the Byzantine emperor, it was only natural that he would send Cyril and Methodius. They set out in 863 with the blessing of both the state and the church.

German missionaries of the Holy Roman Empire had been working in Moravia for some years. However, they were not very successful because they insisted that all instructions be done in Latin, the official language of the church in the Holy Roman Empire. In contrast, the Byzantine Church always used the local language in teaching, liturgy, and other aspects of church life. Building upon their previous knowledge of the language of the

Slavs, Cyril and Methodius not only preached in the local language but actually developed an alphabet for Slavonic language; this would eventually become the Cyrillic script still used today. They also translated the scriptures and used the local language in developing a Slavonic liturgy. Cyril and Methodius laid the foundations for the future Slavic Christianity.

However, the mission approach of the brothers was opposed by the neighboring German bishops. In order to reinforce their authority, Cyril and Methodius went to consult with the pope. Pope Hadrian II endorsed the Slavonic liturgy and supported their approach. Unfortunately, Cyril died in Rome, and so Methodius returned by himself, now an archbishop, to continue their work in Moravia. Despite papal support, political and church opposition from the Holy Roman Empire landed Methodius in prison for two years. Later he returned to Rome, where the new pope again supported his authority and approach. However, constant opposition from the rival German missionaries and bishops stifled the work of the successors of Methodius in Moravia. The innovative and dedicated mission efforts of the Byzantine Church, however, did bear immediate fruit in Bulgaria and established lasting roots for Slavic Christianity.

John Paul II, the first Slavic pope, described the significance of Cyril and Methodius in an encyclical letter (1985) in this way:

> The work of evangelization which they carried out as pioneers in territory inhabited by Slav peoples contains both a model of what today is called "inculturation" or the incarnation of the Gospel in native cultures and also the introduction of these cultures into the life of the Church. (SA 21)

By the year 907 the gospel had spread across Asia, possibly as far as Japan and Korea. The fall of the T'ang dynasty ended the first Christian moment in China, but the faith of Turkish and Mongol peoples in central Asia would be a source of mission in the future. By this time, half of the Christians in the world lived as a minority under Muslim rule—from Persia and Armenia, through Palestine and Egypt, as far as Spain and Portugal. The Byzantine Church not only was strong in Asia Minor but also had established roots in Bulgaria and Russia. In the West the Christian faith was embraced by most peoples of Europe except for those of

Scandinavia, Prussia (present-day Ukraine), and Lithuania. The ancient homes of Christianity in Ethiopia and India maintained that tradition although they were fairly isolated from the rest of the Christian world.

During this period from 313 to 907, ordinary baptized Christians were no longer the primary agents of mission. Rather, the growing number of men and women who sought a more distinct and austere Christian life in the various monastic movements became the main instruments of mission. Even though they were not founded for mission, "their implicitly missionary dimension began to spill over into explicit missionary efforts" (Bosch 1991, 233). They "saved," strengthened, and spread the Christian faith through their witness and work. Monks and nuns inspired Christians and others around the world. At the same time, mission became associated more with a particular vocation than with baptism in general. How do we today encourage and support *both* the particular (ordained, religious and lay) missionary vocation *and* the general baptismal responsibility for mission?

As for the first snapshot from this period, the story of Alopen and the East Syrian monks in China illustrates how the Christian faith can be presented within a context of other faiths. On the one hand, it was essential to be true to the Christian faith. At the same time, God was presented as a "wind" and "life-giving breath," so that others could understand. Second, the example of Cyril and Methodius points to the importance of presenting the gospel in the language and culture of the people, whether these are people in another part of the world or teenagers in our parish. The necessity and challenge of finding the appropriate way of witnessing to and proclaiming God's reign in religious and cultural worlds outside our own continue to be central issues for mission today.

Both of these glimpses at mission point to the ambiguous and dangerous association between mission and politics. On the one hand, civil leaders such as the Chinese or Byzantine emperors facilitated missionary efforts. But on the other hand, the Chinese dynasty after T'ang and the Holy Roman Empire threw up obstacles to mission. The story of Cyril and Methodius also illustrates the sad lesson of how rivalries and divisions within Christianity can seriously harm the witness and work of mission. From this perspective, they are regarded as the patrons of ecumenism (Ellsberg 1997, 293). In the words of Pope John Paul II, the two brothers were "the authentic precursors of ecumenism, inasmuch as they wished to eliminate effectively or to reduce any divisions, real or only apparent, between the individual communities belonging to the same Church" (SA 14). How do we present the gospel through a common witness of all Christians in our parish and diocese today?

Mission and the Mendicant Movement (1000–1453): Preachers, Third Orders, and Beguines

At the beginning of the second millennium the church was in a very difficult state. Externally, it found itself hemmed in on all sides by Muslim political rule, and mission was almost nonexistent. The Holy Roman Empire and a strong papacy in Rome were developing a unity between the church and state, or what would be called Christendom, in Western Europe. Together they mounted a series of military crusades against the Muslims in the Middle East and against those considered heretics in Europe. Military conquest accompanied by forced baptisms occurred in Scandinavia and Prussia, and the Inquisition was instituted to deal with heretics. Internally, the church in the West in the year 1000 was facing serious problems due to the influences of wealth, power, and clericalism. Most of the rest of the Christian world was simply trying to survive under the rule or threat of Muslims. During this period (as in others), the renewal of mission reinvigorated the church, but it did not come primarily from the monastic orders. The Franciscans, Dominicans, and other new movements provided this spark within the church of the West. Other agents of mission led the Byzantine/Orthodox Church in reaching out to the Russians and the East Syrian Christians to the Mongols, Turks, and Chinese (for a second time).

This time period was marred by two schisms. The story of Cyril and Methodius revealed some of the tensions between the church and state of the Holy Roman Empire (Latin West) and the Byzantine Empire (Greek East). Through a very unfortunate event in 1054, some officials of these two churches mutually excommunicated each other, but "the straw that broke the camel's back" between them occurred when crusaders from the Latin West sacked the sacred city of Constantinople in 1204. The second schism, that of the West in the fourteenth century, was a result of church-state power struggles. The election of two and later three rival popes pointed to deeper problems within the church. The fall of Constantinople to Muslim forces in 1453 marked the end of eleven hundred years of the Byzantine Empire and the end of this moment of Christian mission.

Francis of Assisi: Encountering the Muslim Sultan

In contrast to the crusades and forced baptisms, the spirit and motivation for true Christian mission during this period came out of a religious revival. Rather than coming from the monks and nuns, the laity took the lead in reforming the church by searching for ways to live the gospel life as Jesus did. This often involved popular preaching, voluntary poverty, traveling, and mendicancy (begging for sustenance). The most well-known person of this movement is Francis of Assisi.

When Francis was born in the late twelfth century in the little village of Assisi in central Italy, the church was caught in a corrupt web of wealth and power. Secular leaders often appointed priests and bishops, who then owed them money and allegiance in return. After a number of life-changing events (imprisonment in a neighboring city, a serious illness, and an encounter with a leper), Francis left behind the material wealth of his father and the social prestige of his mother in order to imitate the poverty and life of Christ. While in deep prayer, Francis received the message from God, "Francis, go and repair my church!" At first, he interpreted this as literally repairing a local chapel, but within three years Francis and his companions were "repairing the church" by witnessing to and preaching Christ far beyond Assisi.

One of the most intriguing and less widely known stories of Francis concerns his encounter with a Muslim sultan. After several failed attempts to travel to Muslim lands, Francis finally arrived at the crusaders' camp outside the city of Damietta, strategically situated at the mouth of the Nile River. Francis and his companion, Brother Illuminato, crossed the battle lines and were received by

Sultan Al-Malik al-Kamil as persons of peace, not of the sword. One writer of Francis's life described the event in this way:

> The sultan honored him as much as he was able, and having given him many gifts, he tried to bend Francis' mind toward the riches of the world. But when he saw that Francis most vigorously despised all these things as so much dung, he was filled with the greatest admiration, and he looked upon him as a man different from all others. (Thomas of Celano 1972, 277)

After several days of conversation, Francis and Illuminato were safely escorted back to the crusaders' side. The sultan also granted them and other Franciscans safe passage through the Holy Land. This amazing event speaks of Francis's integrity and character and of the sultan's hospitality and openness.

The Franciscan Rule, which Francis wrote in 1221, presented two approaches to non-Christians, depending on the particular context: (1) Christian presence and witness, and (2) open and explicit proclamation of the gospel. If the members of his order found themselves in circumstances similar to Francis's encounter with the sultan, he encouraged them not to begin with arguments and disputes. The importance of witness for whatever form mission takes is captured by the popular phrase attributed to Francis: "Preach always, and if necessary use words." Furthermore, Francis was so impressed by the Muslim periodic call to prayer throughout the day that he proposed something similar for Christians. At a time when Christians and Muslims were at war, it is striking and inspiring that Francis of Assisi approached the Muslims in such a nonviolent and open way, while remaining a very faithful Christian, and that the sultan received him in the same spirit.

Beguines: Lay Women in Mission at Home

Many women were involved in this movement of renewal. Clare of Assisi was the first woman to join Francis formally. She is credited with reforming the contemplative life of cloistered women's communities through her founding of the Poor Clares. The sisters depended on the providence of God on a daily basis rather than on endowments. Third Orders also developed as groups of lay men and women affiliated themselves with the mendicant movements and visions while continuing to live in their regular daily situations. Elizabeth of Hungary, who opened hospitals and served the sick and lepers herself, belonged to that stream of the Franciscan movement which would evolve into the Third Order Franciscans. Catherine of Siena of the Dominican Third Order attracted many people even in her youth because of her deep mystical spirituality and her service to the poor, prisoners, and victims of the devastating plague that would claim the lives of one-third of Europe's population. Her dictated writings were so highly regarded that she is one of three women (along with Teresa of Avila and Thérèse of Lisieux) named a doctor of the church.

Another even more striking innovation for women in mission emerged during this religious renewal in the form of the beguine movement. Individual women yearned to live a more intentional spiritual life within their household, beyond the models of cloistered convents and the third orders. Eventually, a loose network of such women developed. They supported themselves and wore a common dress of gray, similar to early Franciscans. Since the church was preoccupied with the threat of heresy in such "free-standing" movements, the beguines with time moved under clerical supervision and received official religious and civil recognition. The beguinage—the residence for beguines—became an enclosed circle of cottages in the midst of a town or city, often surrounded by a canal or wall. It included a church and buildings for community work, charitable ministry, and administration. The physical remains of some beguinages can still be seen in Europe today. Also, a number of beguines became widely known for their holiness, mystical visions, and great learning, and several were among the women preachers at this time. After two centuries many beguines joined other more autonomous women's communities, such as the Cistercians, Franciscans, and Dominicans.

The famous mystic Mechthild of Magdeburg was born in Germany in the early thirteenth century (see Ellsberg 1997, 320–22). Rather than getting married or entering a convent, around the age of twenty she joined a beguine community in its life of prayer, simple labor, and service to the poor. She wrote a book that traced both her deep inner spiritual journey and her criticism of church worldliness. Sections of her writings were circulated and drew both a loyal following and a group of detractors. Life became risky for her, so she eventually joined an established Cistercian convent.

Although the movement declined after two hundred years, its greatest impact and influence were probably within the communities the beguines joined. They represented an alternative model for women seeking to live the life of Jesus:

> Living an acceptable form of the apostolic life, they could remain within the boundaries of traditional spirituality; but being laywomen and free of the restrictions imposed upon cloistered nuns, they had the liberty to experiment and break new ground. (Devlin 1984, 189)

While Christianity was strengthened in the West, it had declined in much of the rest of the world by 1453. With the fall of Constantinople under the expansion of Muslim rule, only a few isolated Christian communities remained in the Middle East and across Asia, with the exception of the Saint Thomas Christians in India. Nubia (Sudan) had become Muslim, and the Coptic Christians were struggling under Turkish-Muslim rule in Egypt. Russia and Ethiopia were the only two countries outside of Western Europe with Christian rulers. "The Christian movement thus found itself in a rather lopsided situation. The majority of the world's Christians resided in the European West. The dominant culture of western Europe was virtually synonymous with Latin Christianity" (Irvin and Sunquist 2001, 504).

In the fall semester of 2004 I was describing the encounter of Francis of Assisi with the sultan to students in my class. A young Muslim student from Palestine raised his hand and said that Muslims also knew of this encounter. According to Islamic oral tradition, the sultan told Francis that he was interested in becoming a Christian but was afraid to do so due to the consequences. How surprising that this story of Francis's mission and Muslim openness is still known among Muslims as well as Christians. By the way, that Muslim student was studying Christianity in order to help fellow Muslims understand and appreciate Christians and their faith more fully. This experience in the classroom points to the relevance and challenge of the prophetic witness of Francis. When Christians and Muslims were confronting one another on the battlefield, Francis of Assisi offered an alternative model of presence and witness. What does this mean for us in the age after 9/11 in terms of interreligious dialogue and peacemaking?

This time period of mission has some flashbacks to the earliest days of the church. First, there was a desire to live a gospel lifestyle. The radical lives of poverty of Francis and Clare of Assisi touched many people. The Franciscans and Dominicans, each in their own way, reclaimed Jesus' mission of explicit preaching and linked it with witness. Clare reaffirmed the connection between contemplation and mission. And the sweeping renewal within the church did not come from the monks and nuns but primarily through the laity. The birth of third orders provided a new avenue for men and women to live their Christian faith in their regular daily life, which was the ideal of the early house churches.

Second, the beguines remind us of the strong presence of women in the early church. Since those early years, the role of women in mission had basically been limited to nuns in cloistered communities. The third orders and particularly the beguine movement provided new avenues for combining personal and communal spirituality with ministerial and missional service. The beguines were precursors for women's active (non-cloistered) religious orders and a variety of much more recent lay associations and intentional communities.

Mission was understood and practiced both at home and in faraway places in an almost seamless fashion. The friars of Francis followed his example and the Franciscan Rule of witnessing and preaching, whether in Italy or abroad. Their contemporaries, the Dominicans, were attentive to the need for mission in Europe as well as in Prussia, Hungary, and the Mongol Empire. Communities of Poor Clares died as martyrs in Palestine, Syria, and Libya within forty years of Clare's death.

The Second Vatican Council reminded us that mission cannot be defined geographically. How do we witness and preach with and without words in our neighborhood and in our wider world?

In Chapter 5 we will continue to follow the footsteps of the church through its history and to learn from the successes and failures of the pilgrim people of God as they strive to be a part of God's mission.

Questions for Reflection

1. In light of what you've read, imagine one snapshot that is most relevant to your understanding of how mission is practiced (a) in your parish and (b) in your diocese.
2. What person, movement, or image is inspiring and enriching for your personal understanding of mission?
3. What did you find most surprising and/or most challenging in this chapter?

Suggestions for Further Reading

Bevans, Stephen B., and Roger P. Schroeder. *Constants in Context: A Theology of Mission for Today.* Maryknoll, NY: Orbis Books, 2004. Chapters 3–5. More detailed background regarding mission during this period of history.

Ellsberg, Robert. *All Saints: Daily Reflections on Saints, Prophets, and Witnesses for Our Time.* New York: Crossroad, 1997. Short inspirational biographies about important men and women in Christian history and their relevance for today.

Irvin, Dale T., and Scott W. Sunquist. *History of the World Christian Movement.* Vol. 1, *Earliest Christianity to 1453.* Maryknoll, NY: Orbis Books, 2001. A very detailed, important, and inclusive study of Christian history written in collaboration with authors from around the world.

John Paul II. *Apostles of the Slavs (Slavorum Apostolorum).* Encyclical letter to the universal church for the eleventh centenary of the apostolic work of Saints Cyril and Methodius, copatrons of Europe, 2 June 1985. Washington, DC: United States Catholic Conference, 1985.

Norris, Frederick W. *Christianity: A Short Global History.* Oxford: One World, 2002. Chapters 1–4. Concise, easily read, insightful history of Christianity.

Smith, Susan E. *Women in Mission: From the New Testament to Today.* Maryknoll, NY: Orbis Books, 2007. Chapters 1–4. Excellent ground-breaking study of women in mission.

5

Mission from Columbus to the Fall of the Berlin Wall (1492–1989)
• •
Prophets, Jesuits, Missionary Societies,
and New Approaches

Having walked through the first three periods of mission in the last chapter, we continue our stroll through the fourth, fifth, and sixth periods of mission in this chapter. (For a more detailed treatment of these three time periods, see Bevans and Schroeder 2004, chaps. 6–8.) We begin with the events surrounding the arrival of Christopher Columbus in the Americas in 1492 and conclude with the fall of the Berlin Wall in 1989, which many historians consider the end of the twentieth century. Both events symbolize a major shift in both world and Christian history. In Chapter 4 we saw how Christianity spread from Jerusalem fairly quickly and extensively through Asia, Africa, and Europe. However, by 1453 the majority of Christians lived in Europe, with notable presence also in Ethiopia, India, and Russia. In this chapter the Christian faith will shift from being the religion of a European majority to a worldwide religion.

Becoming familiar with our past enables us to understand our present and then move into the future. How have we become the church we are today? How has mission continued to change and adapt in different contexts? What people, events, and movements from our history can renew us today, not by reliving the past but by being inspired and challenged by it? What are the constant threads through the changing contexts that can help us to understand what mission means today?

Mission in the Age of Discovery (1492–1773): Conquistadors, Prophets, and Jesuits

With the fall of Constantinople, Europe felt even more closely boxed in by the Muslim domain. After the reforms of the mendicants and others, the church again found itself preoccupied with wealth, politics, and internal problems. Reform and division shook Christianity in the sixteenth century through the Protestant Reformation, the Catholic Reformation, and the Anabaptist Reformation (see Norris 2002, 153–57, 162–71). In the following century the Thirty Years' War, considered "one of the bigger blots on Christian history in Europe" (ibid., 176), began as a religious conflict between Catholics and Protestants and ended as a nationalistic, political, and economic affair. Other events in this period shaped the history of Christianity and the world even more drastically, as European ships opened up new avenues, first along the coast of Africa and on to Asia, and second across the Atlantic to the Americas.

With the two major navigational and economic powers of Spain and Portugal disputing their claims over the new lands, the pope drew a dividing line from north to south, which eventually put Brazil, Africa, and Asia under Portugal's domain, and the rest of the Americas and the Philippines under that of Spain. Also, because the church was not in a position to direct the missionary efforts in these new lands on its own, the pope created a patronage agreement that gave the two royal governments the rights and responsibilities for mission. These two actions illustrate the close (and dangerous!) identification of church and state as a single Christendom and the overlapping goals of colonialism and mission. Back home, Spain and Portugal succeeded in removing the final foothold of seven hundred years of Muslim rule in Europe in the same year as Columbus's "discovery" of America. Soon the optimism from their successful re-conquering of the Iberian Peninsula turned toward conquering new lands and peoples. One of the worst tragedies in human history was the creation of a massive trans-Atlantic slave trade. An estimated twenty-four million Africans were taken from their homes into slavery over a four-hundred-year period. As many as twelve million may have died in the march and in the coastal holding cells/castles even before being loaded on the ships for transportation to the Americas.

Within this overall situation, many missionaries traveled from Europe to these new lands for the sake of the gospel, and the vast majority were Catholics. This fourth period of mission ended in 1773 with the suppression of the Jesuit Order, which played a major role in mission at this time. Since there was a stark difference between mission in the Americas and in Asia, we shall look at a snapshot from each.

Bartolomé de Las Casas: Prophet in the Americas

From the Caribbean the Spaniards moved to the continent and eventually conquered the two mighty empires of the Aztecs and Incas, of New Spain (Mexico) and the Peruvian region respectively, as well as the descendants of other ancient cultures like the Mayans and Toltecs. Before the arrival of the Europeans about 15 percent of the world population lived south of the Rio Grande River. An estimated sixty million indigenous people died during the course of this invasion as a result of sicknesses (for which they had no immunity), armed conflict, hard labor, malnutrition, and cultural disintegration (see Gutiérrez 1993, 461–64). The aim of the colonial enterprise was conquest, settlement, and Christianization. To accomplish the second and third goals, the Spaniards established a plantation *(encomienda)* system whereby a settler had the responsibility for teaching the Christian faith to the indigenous people on his property and the right to their labor. This resulted in indentured labor at best and slavery at worst. While many priests collaborated with the official state-church mission of the "sword and the cross," other missionaries did not agree and followed alternative ways of doing *real* mission. We will look at one of these.

When Bartolomé de Las Casas was a young boy in Spain, he heard about the return of Columbus after his discovery of the Americas. Caught up in this excitement, the eighteen-year-old Las Casas traveled to the New World for the first time. He then went to Rome to study for the priesthood, returned to the Americas, and became a chaplain of the Spanish soldiers and settlers in Cuba. He got even more involved in the conquest of the Americas

when he became the owner of a plantation with indigenous indentured laborers. But then something turned him upside-down!

On the nearby Caribbean island of Hispaniola (present-day
Dominican Republic and Haiti), Dominican missionaries spoke
out strongly against the terrible treatment of the indigenous
peoples. Father Antonio Montesinos proclaimed the following
in his sermon before Christmas in 1511 to a Spanish congregation: "You are all in mortal sin! You live in it and die in it! Why?
Because of the cruelty and tyranny you use with these innocent
people." Las Casas experienced a deep conversion when he heard
about the prophetic stance of the Dominicans and when he witnessed this cruelty with his own eyes. He underwent a drastic
change from being a plantation owner to standing up for the
human rights of the indigenous peoples. He joined the Dominicans and eventually became known as the "defender of the Indians."

While Europeans in general considered the indigenous peoples
a lesser race, Las Casas asserted their full humanity. While many
supported the use of force even to baptize the people, he affirmed
their rights of choice and religious freedom. Las Casas did not
mince words in pointing out the sinfulness of what he saw:

> In order to gild a very cruel and harsh tyranny that destroys
> so many villages and people, solely for the sake of satisfying
> the greed of men and giving them gold, the latter, who them-
> selves do not know the faith, use the pretext of teaching it
> to others and thereby deliver up the innocent in order to
> extract from their blood the wealth which these men regard
> as their god. (in Ellsberg 1997, 306)

Las Casas influenced Pope Paul III to write a statement on the
fundamental human dignity of the Indians and King Charles V of
Spain to write new laws to attempt to eliminate the major abuses
occurring in the Americas. Las Casas became bishop in the area
of Chiapas in southern Mexico, but his strong action for the indigenous peoples resulted in a number of death threats to himself
and his eventual resignation as bishop. Nonetheless, his passion
for human rights and social justice continued until his death at
the age of eighty-two.

One disturbing flaw in Las Casas's prophetic stance was his initial support of African slavery, which he considered only from the perspective of its benefits for the native peoples of the Americas. Later he recognized his mistake and directed his attention to fighting on behalf of the indigenous peoples of both the Americas and Africa, becoming one of the first to do so.

Francis Xavier: Missionary in Asia

In contrast to the inland invasion and huge number of European settlers in the Americas, the Portuguese during the same period (1492–1773) established a number of unlinked coastal strongholds/forts in strategic places like São Tomé (West African island), Goa (south of Bombay), Malacca (Malaysia), and Macao (near Hong Kong) (see Map 2). Portugal lacked the finances and land forces of Spain, and some Asian civilizations, such as China and Japan, were able to resist extensive foreign intrusion. It was still colonization, but a less drastic form. Therefore, the missionaries in Asia were not absorbed in a sweeping conquest. The Jesuits, who had been founded by Ignatius of Loyola in 1540 as part of the Catholic Reformation, were initially the main missionaries to go to Asia. Their positive attitude toward human nature and non-Western cultures led to a much more creative and accommodating approach toward mission than that practiced in the Americas at the same time.

Francis Xavier grew up in a small castle in northern Spain, studied at the University of Paris, joined the founding group of Jesuits, and became one of the most famous Catholic missionaries. His passion for God's mission carried him by land and sea over ten thousand miles in ten years. Xavier was responsible for the baptism of perhaps as many as 700,000 (Norris 2002, 149). However, his greatest achievement is not captured in statistics but rather in his missionary passion and his missionary "conversion." After an initial period in the Portuguese settlement of Goa (south of Bombay/Mumbai), Xavier did extended missionary work among the pearl-fishing Paravas people on the southeast coast of India (south of Tranquebar; see Map 2). He taught the youth prayers, the Creed, and the Ten Commandments in their own language, and they were set to music The young people, in turn, taught

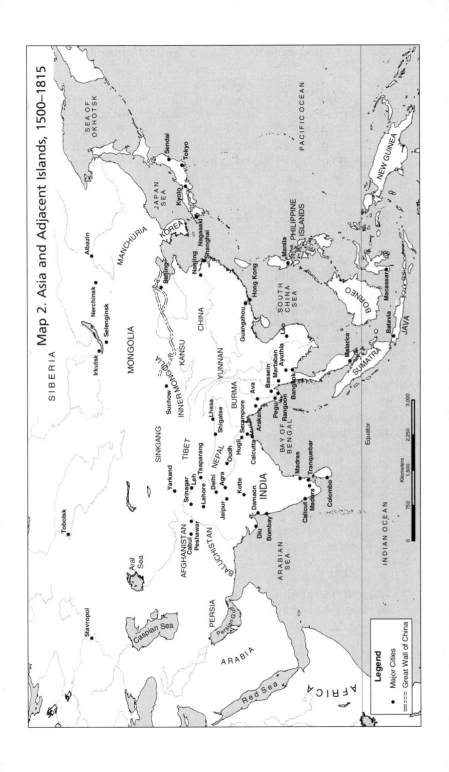

Map 2. Asia and Adjacent Islands, 1500–1815

other villagers. Xavier baptized many, especially among the poor and low caste. He also wrote against the scandalous behavior and the mistreatment of Indians by the colonists. From India, Xavier traveled and worked in Malacca (Malaysia) and parts of present-day Indonesia for two years. During this first part of his missionary life, Francis certainly loved the people, but he didn't appreciate their way of life or their culture, which was so different from the castles and universities of Europe. But then something very important happened after his arrival in Japan after 1549. He wrote the following:

> It seems to me that we shall never find . . . another race to equal the Japanese. They are a people of very good manners. . . . They like to hear things propounded according to reason; and, granted that there are sins and vices among them, when one reasons with them, pointing out that what they do is evil, they are convinced by this reasoning. (in Bevans and Schroeder 2004, 185)

Francis Xavier respected the Japanese society and culture and tried to adapt himself and his work to Japanese ways of living and thinking. Xavier realized that God was somehow already present in the Japanese people, and he wanted to build on those foundations. He shifted his attention from the common folk to the local feudal-like lords whose favorable stance could open up the opportunity for the spread of the Christian faith to others. Two of the Japanese who were baptized by Xavier contributed significantly to these early mission efforts. The first, who had been a Buddhist monk, was extremely helpful in bridging the cultural and religious gap between the missionaries and the Japanese. The second, a wandering professional minstrel who became the first Japanese Jesuit brother and took the religious name of Lourenço, was very instrumental in spreading the gospel through music. Because Francis Xavier was respectful of their culture, Japanese converts participated very soon in mission work among their own people. After Xavier's twenty-seven months in Japan, about a thousand people were baptized. Leaving other missionaries in Japan, Xavier dreamed of going to China, but he became seriously ill on the ship and died at the age of forty-six on an island off the coast of China.

Other Jesuit missionaries followed the lead of Francis Xavier and carried out this approach in even more profound ways in Asia. Outstanding examples include Matteo Ricci, who entered the world of Confucianism in China; Robert de Nobili, the caste system in India; and Alexandre de Rhodes, the language and culture of Vietnam. In 1927, Pope Pius XI proclaimed Francis Xavier, together with Thérèse of Lisieux, a patron of missionary work.

By 1773 Christianity had succeeded in moving beyond Europe, Russia, Ethiopia, and the Saint Thomas Christians of India to the Americas, the Philippines, small communities throughout the rest of Asia, and a few coastal peoples of sub-Saharan Africa (particularly in present-day Congo). However, colonialism, racism, and the political-economic decline of Spain and Portugal hampered the church in the Americas. Misunderstanding and conflict between different missionary orders, between different parts of the Catholic Church, and between the church and civil leaders (particularly the emperors of China and Japan) dampened the promising future for Christianity in much of Asia. The suppression of the Jesuits in 1773 marked the end of this period of mission. By the year 1800 there were probably only about three hundred Catholic missionaries left in the world.

Las Casas is a powerful example of how concerns for human rights and social justice are intimately a part of mission. In his particular context he confronted blatant racism, prejudice, and violence toward the indigenous peoples of the Americas and of sub-Saharan Africa. Not only the colonists, but also some priests and theologians, were convinced that these peoples were naturally inferior, not even human. The prophetic voice of Las Casas was directed to civil and church leaders both in the Americas and in Europe. He was not only concerned with ending this injustice on a day-to-day basis, but he also addressed the plantation and colonial systems themselves, that is, the underlying structures and principles that caused the day-to-day injustice. Las Casas addressed racism within the church itself, as a theologian, as the bishop of

Chiapas, and by influencing the pope. Only three indigenous Americans were ordained in three hundred years because indigenous peoples were not considered worthy of ordination; their worthiness for the reception of the Eucharist was even questioned by some. Closer to our own time, African Americans could not study in Catholic seminaries in the United States until the 1920s. What are the issues of injustice, inhumanity, violence, and particularly racism that we need to address not only in our society, nation, and world but also in our parish, diocese, and church today?

We see in Las Casas the need continually to confront prejudice and racism within ourselves. Las Casas was open to God's grace, which turned his life upside-down *twice*, first in facing his prejudice against native Americans and second against Africans. And the great missionary Francis Xavier had to come to a realization of the value of the ways of life and the cultures of the peoples among whom he worked. Both of these missionaries had conversion experiences, and they became better missionaries because of that. In the 1990s a missionary congregation in the United States produced a video of Hispanic, African American, and Vietnamese American confreres talking about their experiences of racism and ethnocentrism *within* the religious community. The congregation used this video as part of a process to address racism within the religious community itself before addressing issues of racism in ministry with others.

Xavier is also a wonderful example of one who combined his burning passion for proclaiming the gospel with the need to inculturate or accommodate it to the culture and context in which he preached. We saw a similar pattern in Chapter 4 with the East Syrian monks in China and Cyril and Methodius among the Slavs. The attitude of Xavier and other Jesuits in Asia opened the door for Asians to become co-workers and fellow Jesuits, which was extremely rare in the Americas at this time. In these two snapshots we see both the sin and the grace of the church. Jesus described the kingdom of God as going out to the crossroads and inviting everyone to a big wedding feast (Mt 22:2–10). The stories of Bartolomé de Las Casas and Francis Xavier inspire and challenge us to play a part in God's plan to invite all peoples to such a banquet, not just in heaven, but on earth as well. We recall the image of table fellowship.

Mission in the Age of Progress (1792–1914):
Civilizers, Evangelizers,
and Volunteer Societies

After 1773 the state of mission in the Catholic Church was dismal, and it would get worse before getting better. By this time the banner was passing from Spain and Portugal to France as the leading Catholic nation. However, the French Revolution of 1789 and the wars of Napoleon until 1815 put a strangle hold on the French church. The pope and the Sacred Congregation for the Propagation of the Faith, which had been established in 1622 to direct Catholic mission efforts, were basically under house arrest. Religious orders were suppressed, and religious authority and even religion itself were called into question. After Napoleon, the church was preoccupied with struggles between liberal and conservative movements. In time the Catholic Church returned to the matters of mission. However, Protestantism represented the bulk of Christian missionary movement during this fifth period of mission. The name of William Carey and the foundation of the Baptist Missionary Society (BMS) in England in 1792 mark the beginning of the nineteenth-century missionary movement. Of the thousands engaged in mission during this period, it is important to note that by 1890 women represented 60 percent of the Protestant missionaries from the United States (Bevans and Schroeder 2004, 218).

The understanding and practice of mission, for both Catholics and Protestants, are linked with a movement sweeping the globe— another wave of colonialism. The three C's of colonialism were Christianity, commerce, and civilization. Such innovations as the steam engine, railroads, and electricity fueled economic and social development in Europe (and later in North America) during this period, which would become known as the Age of Progress. Along with others, missionaries became ambassadors for bringing these developments to the rest of the world, but others did not always experience this as progress, since they continued to be treated as inferiors. The beginning of World War I in 1914 marks the end of this nineteenth-century period of mission optimism.

Samuel Ajayi Crowther:
African Missionary to Africans

The year 1792 is considered the beginning of this period of Christian mission because of the initiative of William Carey, mentioned above. However, it was also significant because in that same year the first Africans arrived in Freetown in Sierra Leone (West Africa), a settlement established for freed slaves. The first eleven hundred African settlers had been plantation workers in the United States, soldiers in the British army, or farmers in Nova Scotia. They brought their own preachers to their community, which would become a center of mission for fellow Africans. Our snapshot is taken of the one who led them, Samuel Ajayi Crowther, considered by many as "probably the most widely known African Christian of the nineteenth century" (Walls 2002, 155).

Crowther had been captured in Yorubaland (present-day Nigeria) and was to be brought to the Americas as a slave. Fortunately, he was rescued from the slave ship by a British naval squadron and taken to Freetown in 1822. The very gifted Crowther became a teacher and, after study in England, was ordained an Anglican priest. Back in Freetown he led an all-African mission effort back to the area of his birth. He was consecrated a bishop in 1864. English was used in worship in Sierra Leone, but Crowther introduced the use of his local language, Yoruba, among his own people in worship and he took the lead in translating the Bible. Crowther was committed to the gospel and calling people to true conversion, but at the same time he respected African culture. It is not surprising that he was a voice against slavery and that he also developed a good working relationship with the Muslims:

> He enjoyed courteous and friendly relations with Muslim rulers, and his writings trace various discussions with rulers, courts and clerics, recording the questions raised by Muslims, and his own answers, the latter as far as possible in the words of Scripture: "After many years' experience, I have found that the Bible, the sword of the Spirit, must fight its own battle, by the guidance of the Holy Spirit." (Walls 2002, 162)

Change in the wider world affected these developments in West Africa. In the 1870s colonialism became more intense and imperialistic as the spirit of nationalism and the rights and responsibilities for spreading political, economic, and religious domination over others grew dramatically. One representative event became known as the "scramble for Africa." In 1884–85 the German statesman Otto von Bismarck gathered representatives of European colonial nations, particularly England and France, in Berlin to draw lines through an African map to divide up the continent, mostly sight unseen, for their own purposes. This imperialistic spirit was reflected in the new missionaries from Europe, who were "children of their time." The new missionaries who came to West Africa did not support Crowther, and eventually they pushed the aging bishop aside and replaced him with a European bishop. This caused tension and eventual division within the African Christian community.

Despite the regretful end to this story, the promising mission of Crowther should not be forgotten. "The legacy of Samuel Ajayi Crowther, the humble, devout exponent of a Christian faith that was essentially African and essentially missionary, has passed to the whole vast church of Africa and thus to the whole vast church of Christ" (Walls 2002, 164).

Daniel Comboni:
Regeneration of Africa by Africans

Emerging from the chaos of the French Revolution and the Napoleonic Wars, the Catholic Church in France began to recover the vision and means for mission again. The Jesuits were restored in 1814; the Congregation for the Propagation of the Faith was reconstituted in 1817; and Gregory XVI, who became pope in 1831, brought to the papacy his missionary commitment from his earlier days as the prefect for the Congregation for the Propagation of the Faith. Even before these events, a woman who as a ten year old had aided clergy in hiding during the French Revolution, became Sister Anne-Marie Javouhey. She founded the Sisters of St. Joseph Cluny in 1807 and initiated the nineteenth-century Catholic mission efforts in Africa. Hundreds of new religious congregations of men and women were founded during this period, and many of them were devoted to missionary work. We shall focus on one of the founders.

The Italian Daniel Comboni first went to the Sudan as a missionary through the Mazza Institute in Verona near his home. After a short time he had to return home due to the closure of the mission effort and his own poor health. Both of these events reflect the serious health hazards that European missionaries faced. Malaria in particular and the lack of appropriate medicine contributed to the high mortality rate. Comboni's ongoing passion for Africa coupled with his abhorrence of slavery prompted him to become involved in efforts to ransom African slaves and bring them to Europe for education.

In 1864 he drew up his "Plan for the Regeneration of Africa," which included establishing centers in Africa for training both Europeans and Africans for mission work. The accompanying motto of "Save Africa through Africa" paralleled the vision and practice of Crowther in another part of the continent with Africans being missionaries to Africans. The institute Comboni founded to carry out this vision would lead to the foundation of two missionary congregations of men and women. Comboni was unsuccessful in his efforts to get the whole church to embrace mission to Africa at the First Vatican Council in 1870, because that council was preoccupied with other concerns and was cut short due to political change in Italy. Despite such setbacks, Comboni worked tirelessly to promote his plan for Europeans and Africans to do mission together. Often this involved defending the human dignity and ability of Africans, especially during and after the 1870s, when imperialism and racism became stronger. The depth of his life commitment to proclaiming the gospel in Africa is captured in his own words from 1872:

> As for me and my missionary colleagues, you know that we joyfully consecrate our lives to the good of this part of the world, still almost unknown and lying in such great misery, so that we may win it for Christ. Our only plan, which, with God's help and with all the means of human prudence and caution, we want to carry out, is this "Africa or death." (in Tescaroli n.d., 61)

Comboni became a bishop and was named the vicar apostolic of Central Africa in 1877. Four years later he died in Africa before he was able to carry his plan further. However, he was a passionate inspiration for proclaiming the gospel and a prophetic voice for the dignity of Africans and their rightful place in the church and mission. Comboni was canonized 5 October 2003.

By 1914 Christian missionaries had reached most parts of the world, except for places like Tibet, Afghanistan, Nepal, and the interior of Papua New Guinea. Usually at least a small community of baptized Christians remained as the fruit of those efforts. Catholics of the United States had begun to join the steady stream of their fellow citizens of Protestant churches in missionary efforts outside the country. At first, they went as members of missionary communities founded in Europe, such as the older communities of Redemptorists, Passionists, Franciscan Sisters, and Jesuits, or as members of the more recently founded Franciscan Missionaries of Mary, Society of the Divine Word, and Holy Spirit Missionary Sisters. In 1908 both the United States and Australia were removed from the official list of mission countries. In response, the Maryknoll Priests and Brothers (Catholic Foreign Mission Society of America) was founded in 1911, and the Maryknoll Sisters (Mission Sisters of St. Dominic) the following year.

In the first part of this chapter we had the powerful examples, first, of Las Casas speaking and acting prophetically on behalf of the human dignity of the indigenous peoples of the Americas and of Africa, and second, Francis Xavier in another way affirming the human dignity of the Japanese. The snapshot view of Daniel Comboni during this period picked up on this aspect of mission and pushed the question of Africans in turn being missionaries. Shifting our view to another part of the Christian world, Samuel Ajayi Crowther was an excellent example of this vision in reality. This view is founded on the beliefs of the early church that all Christians are equally members of the church and committed to carrying on Jesus' mission. The words and actions of Crowther, Comboni, and other Christian men and women confronted the evils of the nineteenth-century world of imperialism, paternalism, and racism. How does paternalism and prejudice creep into and undermine our desire to understand and practice mission in the twenty-first century in terms of mutuality? How do we view priests, brothers, sisters, and Catholics from other countries who are now serving in and/or are members of our parish?

Gambian-born Catholic historian Lamin Sanneh, a convert from Islam, confronts the image that Africans were passive victims in the colonization and evangelization processes (Sanneh 1991, 2). Africans and other colonized peoples continued to be active subjects in shaping their own history and their own Christian faith. The twentieth century (discussed below) is known as the Christian Century of Africa because the number of Christians shifted from 10 to 360 million from 1900 to 2000. And Africans not only witnessed to their faith to fellow Africans but to other peoples of the world as well. The roots of this movement can be traced to the nineteenth century. Sanneh affirms that the word of God has a power of its own. Even though missionaries as "children of their time" were generally tied to imperialism and prejudice and in spite of the additional obstacles caused by their personal weaknesses and limitations, the word of God was presented to the people. Translations of the scriptures by Crowther and others provided the means for people to listen and respond, negatively or positively, to that word in their own language. Certainly, missionaries and all Christians have the responsibility to witness to and proclaim the gospel as authentically and truthfully as possible. However, missionaries and Christians of the past and of today should not get too much credit or too much blame.

We can't forget that it is God's word, not our own. We recall the parable of the seed growing while the farmer sleeps. "Night and day, while he sleeps, when he is awake, the seed is sprouting and growing; how, he does not know" (Mk 4:27). What an invaluable lesson and reminder for us today! In mission and ministry we are a part of God's mission. As was pointed out in Chapter 2, this was recaptured in the Second Vatican Council. How can this theology and attitude be a guide and support for Christian parents raising children; for ministers to the elderly, sick, and dying; and for missionaries in very difficult situations today?

Mission in the Twentieth Century (1919–1989): The Emergence of World Christianity

As we move into this sixth and final period of mission, we enter our living memory of church and world history, which is possibly more interesting and seems more relevant for us. World War I (1914–18) shattered the hopes that Europe and the United States had placed in science, "progress," and intelligence to create a better world; it also dashed Christianity's plans to evangelize the world "in this generation." Following this disappointment, Pope Benedict XV published a mission encyclical in November 1919 entitled *Maximum Illud (On Spreading the Catholic Faith throughout the World)*. This signaled a return to the mission agenda and the beginning of the Catholic twentieth-century missionary movement. World War I was followed by an economic depression in the 1930s, the rise of Hitler and Mussolini, and finally, World War II. The horror of what humans can do to one another included the deaths of ten million in Stalin's attempts at the reconstruction of Russia and the creation of the "new socialist man." In World War II, as many as forty-seven million civilians and twenty-five million military personnel perished, including twenty-six million in Russia and six million Jews in the Holocaust (a large part of the nine to eleven million who died in the Nazi persecutions overall). Over two hundred thousand people died in 1945 from the atomic bombs dropped on Hiroshima and Nagasaki, approximately half on the days of the bombings and thousands more later from injuries or radiation-related illnesses. The war spelled the beginning of the end of colonialism and dramatically affected the shape of the world and of mission as well. The 1960s brought additional changes in all areas of life, symbolized in particularly vivid ways in the West by huge public demonstrations in 1968.

Stepping back to the beginning of this period, the Russian Revolution of 1917 marked the entrance of Marxist communism, which spread into Eastern Europe, central Asia, North Korea, and China by 1953, and later to Cuba and Vietnam. The Cold War dominated the world economic and political agendas, and atheistic communism became the persecutor and antagonist of Christianity and its mission. The fall of the Berlin Wall in 1989 marked the end of the Cold War and the mission period under consideration here. However, the rise of the OPEC (Organization of the Petroleum Exporting Countries) nations in the 1970s signaled a new complex alignment of economic, political, and religious agendas and challenges between Christians and Muslims. Within this global context, the twentieth century was a time of tremendous change, tension, rebirth, and growth for the church and mission.

Icons of the Transformation of Mission

Mother Teresa: Presence among the Poor

Before the Second Vatican Council the primary motivations for mission were the salvation of souls and the planting of the church. However, some missionaries saw that mission had to be concerned not only with salvation in the next life but also with bettering the human condition in this life; not only with bringing people into the church but also with caring for and working with people in the world, particularly those most in need. We will look at the snapshot of probably the most widely known missionary of the twentieth century as a representative of this broadening understanding and practice of mission.

Mother Teresa, born in Albania, was called Sister Agnes for the first twenty years of her missionary work as a teacher in India. In 1946 she received a call from God to do something more—to shift from teaching mostly middle-class children to being with the poorest of the poor. She sought and received permission from her congregation to leave the convent and her traditional habit in order to put on a white sari and enter the streets of Calcutta. In particular, her heart was moved by the sight of those left to die in street gutters. She established a home where they would be treated with human dignity as God's children in their final days of life. Other centers of service were eventually set up in India and around the world to care for the most destitute and unwanted. A steady flow of women began joining her new community, the Missionaries of Charity, to be an embodiment of God's love. Mother Teresa expressed her vision in this way:

> God has identified himself with the hungry, the sick, the naked, the homeless; hunger, not only for bread, but for love, for care, to be somebody to someone; nakedness, not of clothing only, but nakedness of that compassion that very few people give to the unknown; homelessness, not only just for a shelter made of stone, but that homelessness that comes from having no place to call your own. (in Ellsberg 1997, 393)

After many years other people around the world became aware of the work and witness of Mother Teresa. Christians and non-Christians heard about her through documentary films and books. She received many awards, including the Nobel Peace Prize in 1979. She then spread the message of God's love through her international travel and the work of her sisters far beyond India. In response to the praise she received for her great works in India, Mother Teresa encouraged and challenged people to do "something beautiful for God" wherever they live and not to be concerned with calling something great or small. "To show great love of God and our neighbor we need not do great things. It is how much love we put in the doing that makes our offering something beautiful for God" (in Ellsberg 1997, 392). The television broadcast around the globe of her funeral in Calcutta in 1997 reflected her international fame and influence. She was beatified in 2003.

Dorothy Day: Prophet of Justice and Peace

Mission work after 1492 was understood in a geographical sense to be activity outside Europe. When the United States was no longer officially considered a mission country after 1908, the main focus of its mission outreach was outside North America. However, in the United States some men's and women's congregations continued the earlier work among Native Americans and African Americans. The Glenmary Society of Priests, Brothers and Sisters was founded in 1937 for "domestic mission" among the unchurched in rural areas. On a worldwide level, in 1931 Pope Pius XI established the Catholic Action movement for laity to address social-economic concerns at home. Coming from another source but in the same spirit, a parallel movement began under the leadership of a Catholic lay woman in the United States.

Dorothy Day has been referred to as the most influential and significant person in the history of U.S. Catholicism (Ellsberg 1997, 519). However, her life started out very differently. Dorothy Day rejected Christianity during her college years in favor of radical social causes. She worked as a journalist in New York and took part in protests. Her turning point or conversion was triggered by her pregnancy (outside marriage) and a staggering sense of being lost. Both factors led her to God and the baptism of her child and herself in the Catholic Church. As a result, her common-law husband left her, and Day searched for a way to reconcile her social commitments with her newfound faith.

In 1932 she met a like-minded man, Peter Maurin, who encouraged her to start the *Catholic Worker* newspaper to address the social problems of the poor and working class. (The paper continues to be sold for a penny today.) The Catholic Worker movement established houses of hospitality for the homeless during the Great Depression and later for the most marginalized of society. Similar to Las Casas, Day addressed the social system itself, which created poverty. Dorothy was such a strong and constant voice for peace and nonviolence that her position almost split the movement. It is quite striking that she combined her radical social commitment with a traditional Catholic spirituality and piety. Robert Ellsberg describes her significance in this way:

> In combining the practice of charity and the call to justice Day represented a type of holiness not easily domesticated, but perhaps of special relevance to our times. . . . Her life was a living parable, focused on what she called the mystery of the poor: "that they are Jesus, and what you do for them you do to Him." (Ellsberg 1997, 521)

Dorothy Day died in 1980, and her case for beatification officially began in 2000.

While most of the avenues of mission for U.S. Catholic laity were within the country, overseas opportunities began to emerge during this same time. A number of individuals went to other countries with men's and women's missionary congregations in the 1920s and 1930s, and the Grail movement of Holland established a U.S. house in 1944. In the 1950s the Women Volunteers for Africa and Lay Mission Helpers of Los Angeles were founded. Lay men and lay women joined Papal Volunteers for Latin America in the 1960s and early 1970s. Lay mission and volunteer programs have multiplied dramatically since Vatican II.

Emergence of World Christianity: Christianity as a World Religion

By 1989 and the fall of the Berlin Wall, Christianity had become a world phenomenon through some surprising shifts. Before World War I, Europe (with its "extension" in North America) and Russia (Orthodox Church) were considered the heartlands of Christianity, but by World War II Christianity was beginning to wane in Western Europe. Meanwhile, under communism in the Soviet Union and the Soviet domination of Central and Eastern Europe, Christianity suffered serious persecutions. By the end of the twentieth century the majority of Christians lived in Africa, Latin America, and Asia. Christians still made up about one-third of the world population, but Christianity's geographical location had shifted from the North to the South. The Catholic Church continued to account for about half the world's Christians, but both Catholicism and Christianity as a whole were being shaped more and more by non-Western Christians—by their numbers, vital faith, ethical values, worship styles, devotional practices, and daily concerns (such as AIDS, global social injustice, war, and famine). Christians of the North were challenged to appreciate what others were bringing to the common table. For many—accustomed to the unchallenged hegemony of Western churches—the change has not come easily. Other major changes have included the emergence of the Pentecostal (or charismatic) movement as the fastest-growing form of Christianity in Asia, Africa, and Latin America, demonstrated by the fact that as many as fifty-five million Africans are members of African Independent Churches.

More about all this in later chapters. For the moment, let us consider the meaning of our two missionary "icons."

Mother Teresa and Dorothy Day incarnated God's mission of love. They saw and served God in the poor and outcasts. Twenty years ago I visited one of the centers of the Missionaries of Charity in the midst of the stark human misery and poverty of Calcutta. It came back to me when I had an encounter a few years later in a Catholic Worker house of hospitality in Chicago for street people who were dying of AIDS. While they shared a strong Christian faith and a total commitment to the poor, these two women responded in different ways. Mother Teresa focused on responding to the people in front of her; her critique of society was implicit. On the other hand, Dorothy Day focused on both underlying social issues and attending to immediate needs through the houses of hospitality. How do the examples of these women challenge us to live and practice the Beatitudes (Mt 5:3–12) and the mission of God's love in our parish and diocese?

Both women did great work, and neither wanted to be put on a pedestal. In her down-to-earth reflection, Mother Teresa stated, "We can do no great things, only small things with great love." When people wanted to work with Mother Teresa in India, she would often tell them: "Find your own Calcutta!" In other words, you don't have to do great works or go far away from home to find and serve God in the poor. Transforming the world through love starts by loving one person who is considered unlovable.

Dorothy Day did not want her strong faith and commitment to justice to be considered relevant only for a "living saint." She came to see that every simple act of love can contribute to building up the body of Christ. How can the commitment of these two persons to God, the church, and the poor inspire and encourage us in our daily situations? What little, single act of love can we do now to contribute to, in the words of Mother Teresa, doing "something beautiful for God"? What does Dorothy Day's passion for justice and nonviolence mean today? How do we pass this on to our children? These two women offer us powerful examples of how we can participate in God's mission of love.

Having traced our history of Christian mission to the twentieth century, we shall now turn our attention in the remaining chapters to mapping out the implications of the current understanding and practice of mission.

Questions for Reflection

1. In light of what you've read, imagine one snapshot that is most relevant to your understanding of how mission is practiced (a) in your parish and (b) in your diocese.
2. What person, movement, or image is inspiring and enriching for your personal understanding of mission?
3. What did you find most surprising and/or most challenging in this chapter?

Suggestions for Further Reading

Bevans, Stephen B., and Roger P. Schroeder. *Constants in Context: A Theology of Mission for Today.* Maryknoll, NY: Orbis Books, 2004. Chapters 6–8. More detailed background regarding mission during the period from 1492 to 1991.

Dries, Angelyn. *The Missionary Movement in American Catholic History.* Maryknoll, NY: Orbis Books, 1998. Excellent study of U.S. Catholic mission history.

Dussel, Enrique, ed. *The Church in Latin America: 1492–1992.* Maryknoll, NY: Orbis Books, 1992. A fine collection of articles by experts organized according to chronology, regions, and topics.

Isichei, Elizabeth. *A History of Christianity in Africa: From Antiquity to the Present.* Grand Rapids, MI: Eerdmans, 1995. An overview of the history of Christianity in Africa until 1960 from the perspective of an African woman scholar.

Jenkins, Philip. *The Next Christendom: The Coming of Global Christianity.* Oxford: Oxford University Press, 2002. An informative and provocative description of the future of Christianity as it shifts from the North to the South.

Norris, Frederick W. *Christianity: A Short Global History.* Oxford: One World, 2002. Chapters 5–8. Short, concise and insightful history of Christianity. Easy reading.

Robert, Dana L., ed. *Gospel Bearers, Gender Barriers: Missionary Women in the Twentieth Century.* Maryknoll, NY: Orbis Books, 2002. A very good ecumenical survey of the mission models of women.

Ross, Andrew C. *A Vision Betrayed: The Jesuits in Japan and China, 1542–1742.* Maryknoll, NY: Orbis Books, 1994. An excellent in-depth study of Xavier, Valignano, Ricci, and the Rites Controversy.

6

Three Documents as Sign Posts for Mission Today

● ●

The Why, Who, and Where of Mission

In earlier chapters we followed the journey of the church in mission. Like a river seeking the sea, the church twists and turns toward its goal of God's fullness and depth. A river both shapes and is shaped by the contour of the land, geological formations, and the work of human hands. So the church and mission shape and are shaped by culture, politics, economics, theology, and the ways we see the world and God. The twentieth century was a time of change, challenge, and rebirth, and it has left us sign posts as we look at mission in the twenty-first century. These sign posts include the three major Catholic documents in the last third of the century:

- *Ad Gentes (Decree on the Missionary Activity of the Church)* from the Second Vatican Council;
- *Evangelii Nuntiandi (On Evangelization in the Modern World)*, an apostolic exhortation by Pope Paul VI; and
- *Redemptoris Missio (On the Permanent Validity of the Church's Missionary Mandate)*, an encyclical letter by Pope John Paul II.

Building upon the foundations and ferment of the Second Vatican Council in AG, both Pope Paul VI's EN and Pope John Paul II's RM elaborated upon and refined the new understanding of mission. It is important to remember that these written

documents did not simply fall out of the sky. Rather, they sur-
faced from the practice of mission on the ground by faithful disciples. Each contributes to the church's understanding of mission
from its own perspective and draws from our rich Christian tradition. Together they offer a fairly complete picture of the challenges the church faces in being faithful to its mission in today's
circumstances. We introduced these three documents in Chapter
2, when we painted the "big picture." Now we need to look at
them more closely.

We begin with a brief review of the understanding of mission
before the Second Vatican Council. Then we offer a detailed description of the perspective and content of the three major Catholic
documents and the three present-day models of mission they represent. Snapshots from Chapters 4 and 5 are included to illustrate
each model. In the second part of the chapter we address the
questions of the motivation, agents, and places of mission.

Mission before Vatican II:
Saving Souls and Establishing the Church

At the risk of oversimplification, one can say that, before the
Second Vatican Council, missionary work was usually understood
in terms of the salvation of individuals through baptism and the
establishment of the institution of the church in "mission lands."
The Gospel states, "The one who believes in it [the good news]
and accepts baptism will be saved; the one who refuses to believe
in it will be condemned" (Mk 16:16). The phrase "outside the
church, no salvation" is attributed to an early church writer,
Cyprian of Carthage, and was important in understanding this
motivation for mission. It is important to realize that the church
did not to teach this in a narrow sense. Indeed, one theologian
who has devoted his life to studying this issue, Jacques Dupuis,
devotes twenty pages to listing what he calls "substitutes for the
gospel." By this he means ways in which theologians, church doc-
tors, councils, and popes showed their confidence that God would
save people who, through no fault of their own, did not have
explicit faith in the terms suggested by Mark 16:16 (see Dupuis
1997, 110–29). Nevertheless, narrow interpretations of this verse

from Mark have been common among many missionaries. It clearly motivated great figures like Francis Xavier, who baptized perhaps as many as 700,000 people. However, as we saw in Chapter 5, he had a change in his understanding when he went to Japan.

Before the Second Vatican Council the practice of ransoming pagan babies was based upon this idea of the salvation of souls. However, the official teaching of the church in the catechism was that baptism takes three forms: water, blood, and desire. The third way provided an avenue for salvation without formal membership in the church and knowledge of Jesus as the Christ. Through the twentieth century skepticism about limiting salvation to explicit knowledge of Christ continued to grow.

The second motivation for mission, of establishing the visible church, was rooted in an ethnocentric evaluation of Western culture as Christian and superior to other cultures. *Ethnocentric* (from the Greek word *ethnos,* "nation" or "people") refers to the almost universal human tendency to evaluate the world from a perspective centered on one's own cultural or national outlook. Even though there was great diversity in Christian history, Western Catholicism seemed to have lost consciousness of that variety. From 1492 onward, many Western missionaries saw themselves as ambassadors of a "higher" Western Christian civilization. We have discussed the dangers of this view as it was practiced in sixteenth-century Latin America and during the colonialism of the nineteenth and twentieth centuries. This ethnocentric model of mission can also be called the Christendom model, that is, a vision of Christianity as essentially rooted in the ideals of medieval Christendom in which only Christians were considered full members of society.

This ethnocentric framework was shaken by two world wars, the Holocaust, and the atomic bomb. It was further dismantled by the rise of such academic disciplines as sociology, anthropology, and the history of religions, which showed that no people or tribe can legitimately claim superiority over others and that no culture can be truly considered fully Christian. The end of colonialism and a growing appreciation of other religions and non-Western cultures spelled the death of ethnocentric theologies of mission. Christianity, it came to be recognized, needs to be expressed from within the positive cultural values of peoples who become Christian.

In the aftermath of World War I and World War II, something new emerged, particularly as some French Catholic thinkers began to question whether France was itself a "mission country." How, they asked, could Christianity be equated any longer with Western culture? This set the stage for a new view of mission, the one that the Second Vatican Council adopted.

Mission as Participation in the Mission of the Triune God

Many books have been written about the Second Vatican Council (1962-65), which was convened by Pope John XXIII, and the way in which it crystallized more adequate approaches to Christian living in our age. We highlight here the three major shifts that defined the new understanding and practice of mission as participation in the mission of God. These shifts shaped the first model of mission that emerged from the deep faith and rich experience of the participants of the worldwide church at the council.

First was the insight that *the Trinity is the center and origin of mission.* The church and thus all Christians find their origin and end in the Trinity, in the mission of God. AG described it this way: God the Father, as the life-giving fountain of love, calls all humanity to the fullness of God's life, not just as individuals but gathered together as a people. This mission of God breaks into history concretely in the Son and continues through the Spirit. Who God is and how God acts is revealed most clearly in Jesus of Nazareth.

> Therefore the Son of God walked the way of a true Incarnation that He might make men and women sharers in the divine nature. He became poor for our sakes, though He had been rich, in order that His poverty might enrich us (2 Cor. 8:9). The Son of Man came not that he might be served, but that He might be a servant, and give His life as a ransom for the many—that is, for all (see Mk. 10:45). (AG 3)

In this account of mission, the church is to be in communion with God's triune life, and its life—as a totality—is destined to be a sign and instrument of God's presence in all of creation. The church reminded itself of the bigger picture described in Chapter 2 as "God's Mission and the Spirit." The church is "missionary by its very nature" (AG 2). "Thus, the church goes from 'having missions' to 'being missionary'" (Schreiter 1994, 117). Or, using the phrase from Chapter 3, *the church doesn't have a mission, but the mission has a church!* This implies that we can also talk about our baptism into a church that is "missionary by its very nature." Furthermore, just as God invites but does not force people to come to God, so the church is to invite and not coerce people to baptism. The church has the responsibility to preach the gospel, but in some circumstances Christian witness and presence may be the only forms of mission (AG 6).

Second, *the understanding of the church's role was clarified.* While the Second Vatican Council portrayed the church in a variety of ways, the primary image developed in its *Dogmatic Constitution on the Church* (LG) is of the church as the pilgrim people of God. Therefore, the church is not a perfect society (without fault), but rather a people on the move toward the reign of God. And while the church may point toward and live from its hope that the reign of God will come, the church in and of itself is not equal to God's kingdom in the full biblical sense of that word. For God's reign is bigger than the church, and the church—in its members, if not in its essence—is part of a fallen world where perfection is sought but not reached. Nevertheless, the church "in Christ," the council says, is the sacrament of salvation (LG 1), whose mission is to point and witness to God's reign (LG 5).

Therefore, the church is to be open to how God is present and moving in the world in the "signs of the times," to use the words of the *Pastoral Constitution on the Church in the Modern World* (GS 4). The church is to be in dialogue with the world. In our study of the Acts of the Apostles, we saw how the early Christian community recognized and followed God's presence in the world of its day in the Samaritans, the Ethiopian eunuch, and the Gentiles. The story of Peter and Cornelius demonstrates this powerfully and clearly. In a very similar way, this openness of Vatican II to God's presence in the world led to a greater appreciation of other Christian denominations, other (particularly non-Western) cultures, and other religions.

Third, *the understanding of other religions was clarified.* Following insights gained from biblical stories such as those just mentioned, the council's *Declaration on the Relation of the Church to Non-Christian Religions* (NA) built upon the teachings in the early church that other religions and philosophies were "preparation for the Gospel" (AG 3). Christians were advised to "enter with prudence and charity into discussion and collaboration with members of other religions" (NA 2). Salvation for all is through Jesus Christ, and Christians are to live and proclaim their faith; at the same time, God is somehow present in other religions "in a way known to God," offering all access to the riches of grace that come from the paschal mystery of Christ's life, death, and resurrection (GS 22).

In addition, the *Declaration on Religious Liberty* (DH) affirms that people in good conscience should be allowed to seek God freely, without force. This speaks against the "sword and cross" approach, as well as other more subtle ways of applying pressure or linking baptism with material or social gain. The conversation of Jesus with the Samaritan woman provides an example of the attitudes and principles necessary for such an encounter. These principles were definitely agreed upon at the council, and the words and gestures of four popes since then show that they are accepted. Nevertheless, many practical questions remain to be resolved concerning these issues as related to mission and to other faiths.

Implications of the Three Missional Principles of Vatican II

What, then, are the implications for mission that follow from these three principles? The Second Vatican Council defined mission as "evangelization and the planting of the Church among those people and groups where she has not yet taken root" (AG 6). But how is this to be done? It is clear that it is not enough to see evangelization as mere proclamation of Christ and establishing the church. Reflecting the nature and mission of God, the church is to do mission in the spirit of service, not imposition.

Since humanity and all creation are graced by God's love, the church is to cooperate with God's mission to bring salvation and reconciliation. Furthermore, the church is to be engaged, as God is, in all aspects of God's creation and world. Mission approaches the world and culture in a positive way. The "secret presence of God" (AG 9) in the tradition and history of every people is like the "seeds of the Word [of God] which lie hidden in them" (AG 11). Christians "can learn by sincere and patient dialogue what treasures a bountiful God has distributed among the nations of the earth" (AG 11).

This means that *mission includes both proclaiming and learning, giving and receiving.* Such an approach opens up many opportunities for a fruitful conversation with other religions and a dynamic relationship between Christianity and all cultures. "But at the same time, let them [Christians] try to illumine these treasures with the light of the gospel, to set them free, and to bring them under the dominion of God their Savior" (AG 11). So humanity and the world are sinful as well and in need of salvation, but the starting point is the loving nature and action of God.

Is this new? Not at all. Precursors of this mission approach include the Greek saints Cyril and Methodius of the Byzantine Orthodox Church, who approached the Slavic language and culture in a very positive manner. In the Middle Ages the third orders and the beguines incarnated God's mission within their daily life and local context. The "converted" Francis Xavier and later Jesuits in Asia respected the "treasures" in the cultures of the Japanese and other Asians. The Nigerian missionary Samuel Ajayi Crowther was able to break the colonial pattern and appreciate African cultures. In going back to its Christian roots, the documents of the Second Vatican Council tapped the richness of several early church writers in speaking about the "seeds of the word" (Justin Martyr) in philosophy and in the world and about other religious ways as "preparation for the gospel" (Eusebius of Caesarea, Clement of Alexandria). Indeed, in all ages the most successful missioners have been those who had an authentic love of the people among whom they worked, and that love showed itself in learning the language, the music, and the ways of life of that people.

The strength of this perspective is the solid starting and end point in God's mission, and the positive attitude to the world—culture, world religions, and creation as a whole. This approach is immersed in God's love and mystery. Its possible weaknesses are that it could be too optimistic, and the importance of Jesus and the church might be underplayed, for example, in relating with other religions.

Mission as Liberating Service of the Reign of God

Representatives of bishops from around the world met in 1974 for the third synod after the Second Vatican Council to discuss evangelization in the modern world. Unable to produce a final document, they gave their conclusions to Pope Paul VI, who published *Evangelii Nuntiandi*, his apostolic exhortation on evangelizing the modern world, in 1975. Rather than starting with the Trinity, Paul VI anchors the mission of the church in the earthly mission of Jesus and his preaching of the kingdom or reign of God. As we saw in Chapter 2 in the section entitled "Jesus and the Reign of God," the preaching, serving, and witnessing to the reign of God "sums up the whole mission of Jesus" (EN 6). In a very powerful and strong statement, the pope says that the reign of God "is so important that, by comparison, everything else becomes 'the rest,' which is 'given in addition.' Only the kingdom therefore is absolute, and it makes everything else relative" (EN 8). Furthermore, this kingdom is absolutely linked with salvation, which Jesus makes available to all those he meets (such as the Samaritan woman), on the condition that they undergo "a total interior renewal . . . by a radical conversion, a profound change of mind and heart" (EN 10).

Just as Jesus was concerned with both physical and spiritual healing, Paul VI teaches that salvation involves "liberation from everything that oppresses man" (EN 9), but he also insists firmly that salvation must not be reduced to merely "temporal activity" or "initiatives in the political and social orders" (EN 32). The appearance of the word *liberation* in an official church document for the first time is due to the influence of what the church was experiencing in Latin America and the link between justice and mission in an earlier bishops synod in Rome in 1971. Although he recognizes the validity of liberation language, his caution reflects concerns regarding some post–Vatican II developments (as perceived, for example, in some developing liberation theologies) that seem to overemphasize this-worldly liberation to the detriment of the holistic liberation of body and soul (see Tomko 2001, 24).

After Jesus' death and resurrection, the pope notes, the disciples were led by the Spirit to continue Jesus' mission, first among the Israelites, and then to carry that mission to the entire world. In these reflections Paul VI elaborates upon the missionary nature of the church and the essential link between the eucharistic table and mission.

> Evangelizing is in fact the grace and vocation proper to the Church, her deepest identity. She exists in order to evangelize, that is to say in order to preach and to teach, to be the channel of the gift of grace, to reconcile sinners with God, and to perpetuate Christ's sacrifice in the Mass, which is the memorial of his death and glorious Resurrection. (EN 14)

Since the church is not a perfect society and not the same thing as the reign of God, the pope reminds us that the church "has a constant need of being evangelized, if she wishes to retain freshness, vigor and strength in order to proclaim the Gospel" (EN 15). Some writers today describe this as mission in reverse, as the evangelized gain new insights into the gospel and offer them to the church as a whole. Evangelization begins, then, with the silent witness of Christian living and later, in response to the questions of those around them, the explicit proclamation of the good news (EN 21-22). If some of these questioners choose to move toward baptism, mission continues, since "it is unthinkable that a person should accept the Word and give himself to the kingdom without becoming a person who bears witness to it and proclaims it in his turn" (EN 24). Remember the example of the women and men "gossiping the gospel" in the early church and the conversation among the catechumenate group in that Chicago parish, presented in Chapter 4.

In the cries for justice, healing, and adequate access to the goods of the world that come from Christians in areas that Western Christians used to call mission lands (for example, Oceania, Asia, Africa, and Latin America), we see an understanding of the gospel that can be described as holistic. Salvation and Christian life are not merely a matter of finding paradise in the world to come. These Christians find concern for this-worldly liberation to be integral to mission, and that new understanding of mission represents a mission in reverse that is helping Christians in the ancient homelands of Western Christianity see new dimensions in the gospel.

EN comes out of this dialogue. Moreover, it deepens and refines the new understanding of mission in introducing the importance of evangelizing the very roots of culture itself (EN 20), taking into account "the unceasing interplay of the Gospel and of man's concrete life, both personal and social" (EN 29), and proclaiming "the liberation of millions of human beings" (EN 30). These latter developments imply that mission is concerned with the transformation of the world and the salvation of society, not just the salvation of individuals. In other words, EN focuses on integral evangelization and integral salvation.

The mission model of the reign of God in EN was clearly evident in, for example, Bartolomé de Las Casas, who dedicated his life to liberating the indigenous peoples of the Americas (and later of Africa) and to defending their human dignity and freedom of conscience before the Christian message. Las Casas was concerned with the salvation of both body and soul.

To take another example, Christians of the East Syrian tradition—Alopen in China and other East Syrian monks engaged in medical care and diplomacy, among others—immersed themselves in their social-political world to witness to and preach the reign of God in a holistic way. Francis of Assisi represents this model due to his prophetic counter-cultural stance to society at his time. He also identified very strongly with the down-to-earth nature of Jesus and his care for and closeness to all of God's creation.

More recent examples of this mission approach include Dorothy Day, Archbishop Oscar Romero, Jean Donovan, Sister Maura Clark, and Dr. Martin Luther King Jr. The 1979 Assembly of the Bishops' Conference of Latin America in Puebla, Mexico, refined its reflection on development and mission, while continuing to affirm the "preferential option for the poor." Likewise, the U.S. Bishops' Conference's 1986 statement, *Economic Justice for All: A Pastoral Letter on Catholic Social Teaching and the U.S. Economy,* pointed to the link between justice and mission.

The strength of this kingdom-oriented model comes from its starting point with the concrete mission of Jesus and its strong basis in scripture. Furthermore, mission is concerned with the whole person and the transformation of society. While the first model was quite optimistic regarding the world, here we see that mission has to be prophetic as it stands up for justice and liberation. The caution is that focusing too exclusively on justice may reduce mission to only secular development work. The role of the church in pointing to the reign of God cannot be lost.

Mission as Proclamation of Jesus Christ as Universal Savior

Twenty-five years after AG and fifteen after EN, Pope John Paul II published the encyclical *Redemptoris Missio* to clarify the question "Why mission?" for people for whom that *why* seemed to be ambiguous or confusing (RM 4). While including the trinitarian foundation of the Second Vatican Council (RM 1, 7, 22, 23, 32) and the reign of God theology of Pope Paul VI (RM 12-20), the underlying and primary motive for mission, according to Pope John Paul II, is the proclamation of Jesus Christ as the universal Savior:

> Why mission? Because to us, as to Paul, "this grace was given, to preach to the Gentiles the unsearchable riches of Christ" (Eph 3:8). . . . The Church, and every individual in her, may not keep hidden or monopolize this newness and richness which has been received from God's bounty in order to be communicated to all humanity. (RM 11)

This perspective is in response to two possible dangers. Those who overstressed the teaching of AG on the holiness of the world, cultures, and religions could advocate that Catholicism teaches that all religions are equally good ways of salvation and that cultures don't need to be transformed by the gospel. Regarding the first point, John Paul II builds upon the teachings of Vatican II and acknowledges that people can be saved outside the church. God's grace through the Holy Spirit "offers everyone the possibility of sharing in the Paschal Mystery in a manner known to God" (RM 6, 10, 28) and the "seeds of the word" are found in human and religious experience (RM 28, 56). At the same time, the pope stresses over and over again in the document that "Christ is the one Savior of all, the only one able to reveal God and lead to God" (RM 5). While interreligious dialogue is an essential element of mission, it "should be conducted and implemented with the conviction that *the Church is the ordinary means of salvation* and that *she alone* possesses the fullness of the means of salvation" (RM 55). The significance of Christ and the church is reaffirmed. As for the second point, regarding culture, John Paul II confirms the importance of incarnating the gospel in all peoples' cultures but adds the caution that we are to avoid compromising "the distinctiveness and integrity of the Christian faith" (RM 52) or overestimating culture (RM 54).

The second danger that John Paul seeks to avoid is placing such emphasis on the reign of God already present in the world that people could see missionaries as simply social workers. Mission activity, the pope warns, could "become something completely human and secularized" and "closed to the transcendent" (RM 17). Some may talk about the kingdom without talking about Christ and "leaving very little room for the church" (RM 17). As above, the pope insists that "the kingdom cannot be detached either from Christ or from the church" (RM 18).

John Paul II was concerned that such misunderstandings were undermining mission "to the nations" (*ad gentes*), that is, to the followers of other faiths and to those of no faith. He distinguished between pastoral care, re-evangelization of those who are no longer Christian (RM 33), and missionary activity in its strictest sense. According to RM, the paradigm for missionary activity is mission *ad gentes*—preaching to those who do not believe in Christ and establishing the church in all parts of the world (RM 34). The geographical sense of this missionary activity is very strong, but the encyclical also talks about mission going "beyond the frontiers of race and religion" (RM 25) and entering into the growing urban areas and new cultural sectors, where Christians work in the areas of communications, peace, development, human rights, ecology, scientific research, and international relations (RM 37).

Prime examples of this model of mission are Saint Paul, who founded many Christian communities, and Saint Francis Xavier, who baptized hundreds of thousands of people across Asia and was named one of the patrons of mission for the Catholic Church. Daniel Comboni is representative of most missionaries of the nineteenth and early twentieth centuries within this approach. While Samuel Ajayi Crowther was mentioned earlier under the trinitarian model, he also was greatly concerned with preaching the salvation of Christ in Africa. The long list of women and men who preceded them with this motivation for mission over the centuries includes the monks and nuns of the Holy Roman Empire of the second mission period and many but not all of the Dominicans and Franciscans of the third period. Mother Teresa would identify herself and her understanding of mission within this model of mission. In December 2007 the Congregation for the Doctrine of the Faith published a paper, entitled *Doctrinal Note on Some Aspects of Evangelization*, to clarify many of the same concerns expressed in RM.

One of the strengths of this model of mission is that it provides strong motivation to be engaged in explicit proclamation. Furthermore, the place of Christ and the role of the church are maintained very clearly. The potential weakness of this approach is that it could lead to an over-spiritualizing of salvation to the detriment of addressing injustice, violence, and poverty in our world today, and also to a closed attitude regarding dialogue and interaction among believers of different religions.

The Why, the Who, and the Where of Mission

Each of these three mission documents and perspectives offers an important model for mission and for being a Christian. On the one hand, there is much overlap among them, while on the other hand, the differences can sometimes be divisive. We saw the sad examples of what happened during the second period of mission with the dispute between the approaches of Cyril and Methodius and the missionaries of the Holy Roman Empire and during the fifth period of mission between Samuel Crowther and the new batch of European missionaries. Today, an exclusive focus on salvation in the next world through baptism could easily conflict with an exclusive focus on salvation in this world through peace and justice programs. Each could accuse the other person or group of ignoring an essential aspect of mission, and in truth, the two exclusive positions are not correct interpretations of the church's understanding of mission today.

The three understandings of mission, as presented in the three official Catholic Church documents, represent a "conversation" that provides the combined wisdom and reflection of the church. Rather than looking at the approaches as either/or propositions, it is better to view them as both/and statements. Taken together, they offer "checks and balances." Such a synthesis may also be considered as a creative tension between two truths, such as (1) God is present and active within all religions, and (2) Jesus Christ is the unique savior of all.

At the same time, most Christians are more at home with one or two of the three perspectives and focus their efforts accordingly. This richness of diverse approaches will ideally contribute to the unity and fullness of Christian mission and identity. For example, in the third period of mission the fruits of the religious revival included the Franciscans, Dominicans, beguines, third orders, and Poor Clares. We now proceed to address the questions of the why, who, and where of mission by drawing on the three models of mission at the beginning of the twenty-first century.

The Why of Mission

The motivation for mission, as developed in the trinitarian model, is based on the image of God as a fountain of love (AG 2). "Mission is the basic and most urgent task of the church, not because without human action so many might not reach some kind of fulfillment, but because to be Christian is to become part of God's life and God's vision for the world" (Bevans and Schroeder 2004, 303). As rain falls on the earth, bears fruit, and then returns to the heavens through evaporation, God's love has brought all people into being and continually is nourishing and drawing them back into God's full embrace. Who we are and what we do is caught up in this movement of our God, a mystery beyond our calculations. As we are loved by God, so we are to "flow" with God's loving action in the world. In other words, "there is mission because God loves people" (Bosch 1991, 392).

From the reign of God perspective we need to do mission to carry on the work of Jesus. The church is "the continuing presence and activity of Jesus in the world, the continuation of Jesus' mission of preaching, serving and witnessing to the kingdom of God" (Bevans and Schroeder 2004, 307). In the clear, straightforward words of Pope Paul VI: "Those who have received the Good News and who have been gathered by it into the community of salvation can and must communicate and spread it" (EN 13). As a community and as individuals, the church is not to be closed in on itself; rather, it prolongs who Jesus Christ is and what he did for the breaking in of the reign of God. Christians do this by witnessing, evoking admiration and conversion, and preaching and proclaiming (see EN 15). Just as the church needs to acknowledge and esteem the seeds of the word in other religions, it is still responsible for enabling people to become aware of God's plan, mission, and presence for the entire human race (see EN 53).

As captured so well in RM, the reason for mission within the third stream is centered on the "clear affirmation that Christ is the one Savior of all, the only one able to reveal God and lead to God" (RM 5). Furthermore, the church is the sign and instrument of this salvation (RM 9), or, to use the language and another essential image of the Second Vatican Council, the church is the universal sacrament of salvation (LG 48; AG 7, 21). The church cannot "deprive men and women of the 'Good News' about their being loved and saved by God" (RM 44). In other words, "all people have a *right* to the fullness of truth, and so the church must be in mission" (Bevans and Schroeder 2004, 324). Mission is a pressing matter because the majority of humanity does not know this or no longer believes. "While respecting the beliefs and sensitivities of all, we must first clearly affirm our faith in Christ . . . a faith we have received as a gift from on high, not as a result of any merit of our own" (RM 11).

Taken together, all three perspectives base their answer to the question "Why mission?" on "the saving love of God, who graciously has called men and women to cooperate in its manifestation" (Bevans and Schroeder 2004, 325). Mission is primarily about who God is and what God is doing with humanity (and all creation). We begin with that mystery, whether our answer is the Trinity, the reign of God, or our savior Jesus Christ. We don't know everything about this mystery of God's saving love, but we Christians do know and have experienced something of the wonders of God. Because of this, we are obliged to be a part of this unfolding movement of God, which is inviting all people, including ourselves, through a lifelong journey of conversion to God's bosom, the complete reign of God, the fullness of truth and salvation in Christ. We cannot hide this truth under a bushel basket for ourselves. The church as that community of faith is to be the all-important sign and instrument pointing to and serving God's purpose, as John the Baptist did for Jesus.

The Who of Mission

In the early church Christians knew that baptism made them full members of the church and likewise collaborators in continuing Jesus' mission. The catechumenate process laid the foundations; house churches, Christian networks, and community prayer and ritual provided building blocks; Christians "gossiped the gospel" and witnessed to their faith (some to the point of death) in their day-to-day circumstances. But the interconnection of baptism, church, and mission became weaker as mission became associated with a select group of individuals. In the sixteenth century this elite corps became known as missionaries. However, in the developments since Vatican II, the Catholic Church has rediscovered its roots in mission.

All three mission documents and approaches clearly emphasize this missionary nature of the church and baptism. AG affirmed that "the whole Church is missionary, and the work of evangelization is the basic duty of the People of God" (AG 35). "Thus it is," according to Pope Paul VI, "that the whole Church receives the mission to evangelize, and the work of each individual member is important for the whole" (EN 15).

In the words of Pope John Paul II, "there is a new awareness that *missionary activity is a matter for all Christians,* for all dioceses and parishes, Church institutions and associations" (RM 2). The responsibility for mission is shared by the pope and bishops (as leaders of the universal and particular/local churches), priests and deacons, members of both active and contemplative religious communities, and lay people. Elaborating on the latter, Pope Paul VI described this role of the laity in their involvement in the world and temporal affairs, in the family "as the center to which the gospel must be brought and from which it must be proclaimed" (EN 71), and in a variety of lay ecclesial ministries. Fifteen years later Pope John Paul II specifically added catechists and "leaders of prayer, song and liturgy; leaders of basic ecclesial communities and bible study groups; those in charge of charitable works; administrators of Church resources; leaders in the various forms of the apostolate; religion teachers in schools" (RM 74).

At the same time, there are those who live out their baptismal call to participate in God's mission by crossing religious, cultural, and economic margins in more deliberate and explicit ways, both near and far from home. Such ordained, religious, and an increasing number of lay Christians are identified as missionaries. Their training and activity usually address specific situations of mission. We have looked at the role of missionaries throughout history and are aware of their inspiring vocation. They emerge from and depend upon the support of their parish, diocese, and/or broader church communities. The diocesan offices of the Society of the Propagation of the Faith and the Holy Childhood Association serve as a link between missionaries and parishes/dioceses. They provide the avenue and animation for supporting missionary efforts through mission appeals, mission education of adults and children, and the annual Mission Sunday in October, among other activities. Missionary societies and organizations likewise draw Catholics into collaboration with their missionary endeavors through magazines, films, fund-raising efforts, education, preaching, and other forms of mission animation. Today, there is the phenomenon of a rapidly growing number of short-term missionaries (especially but not exclusively among the laity), who serve for weeks or months, in contrast to long-term missionaries, who serve for years. Both groups of missionaries bring their own strengths, weaknesses, and gifts, and they need to work well with each other for the sake of mission.

All Christians are called to share in continuing God's mission. As members of the body of Christ, different individuals and groups, such as missionaries, have their own particular gifts and vocations. Through their support of and solidarity with all missionaries, Catholics are reminded of their shared responsibilities for mission both near to and far from home.

Another important aspect of the who of mission is a recognition that the majority of Catholics and Christians, in general, already live in the South. It is projected that "by 2025, Africans and Latin Americans combined will make up about 60 percent of Catholics, and that number should reach 66 percent before 2050" (Jenkins 2002, 195). Accordingly, the majority of the agents of mission are now coming from another part of the world. For example, the largest national group within the international religious order of Divine Word Missionaries (SVD) shifted from German to Indonesian in 1990. From another angle, the increasing presence of Catholics and others coming to the United States from the global South requires a spirit of hospitality and care, but also a spirit of openness and thankfulness for the faith and gifts with which they enrich our church and nation. Some are also coming explicitly as missionaries to respond to pastoral, ministerial, and mission needs in the United States. The receiving church needs to offer them appropriate orientation and mentoring, similar to that given to those working in other countries in mission, and to be open to their witness and service. This is linked with the next question regarding the where of mission.

The Where of Mission

Before Vatican II, mission was defined geographically with the primary mission-sending area consisting of Western Europe, North America, and Australia. The mission-receiving peoples basically lived in the rest of the world, referred to as the missions. During World War II the Frenchmen Godin and Daniel published a pamphlet in which they dared to suggest that France itself had become a mission country (Godin and Daniel 1943). Some twenty years later the Second Vatican Council redefined mission in terms of *God's* mission, which cannot be limited to and confined within humanly determined territory boundaries. Furthermore, just as the universal church is missionary by nature, so every particular or local church (diocese or conference of dioceses) is likewise missionary by nature. As the bishops of the United States stated in their 1986 pastoral statement: "Every local church is both mission-sending and mission-receiving" (TEE 15). The term *missions* was replaced by *mission*. The same shift had occurred within Protestantism as well. The title of the journal *The International Review of Missions* became *The International Review of Mission*. Anglican bishop, historian, and missionary Stephen Neill wrote that "the age of missions is at an end; the age of mission has begun" (Neill 1964, 572). The previous year the mission committee of the World Council of Churches talked about "mission on six continents."

In the twenty-five years after the council, the understanding of mission expanded to explicitly include justice, liberation, interreligious dialogue, the dynamic interaction of gospel and culture for every country, and re-evangelization, particularly in Europe. John Paul II was concerned that this broader approach to mission was diluting the urgency of mission "to the nations," that is, those who do not believe in Christ or where the church is not sufficiently mature. His stress that this is the only missionary activity proper (RM 34) tends to move back to a more geographical understanding of mission. However, the pope tempered this understanding by acknowledging that mission moves "not only geographically but also beyond the frontiers of race and religion" (RM 25) and needs to address the situations of massive urbanization and poverty and what is called the "modern equivalents of the Areopagus" (RM 37; see Acts 17:22-31). This category includes Christians working in the areas of communication in the global village, peace and liberation of peoples, human rights for individuals and minority groups, advancement of women and children, safeguarding creation, and scientific research and international relations.

Several years before John Paul II wrote RM, the U.S. bishops expressed a similar concern. "While we are acutely conscious of our continuing need to evangelize in our own country, that challenge, as great as it is, must never cause us to forget our responsibility to share the good news of Jesus with the rest of the world" (TEE 3). The church of the United States, like every local church, must respond to the challenges regarding mission within its own boundaries *and* participate in mission to all peoples. In regard to the latter, the U.S. bishops highlighted the responsibility of the Society for the Propagation of the Faith and the Holy Childhood Association "to awaken and deepen the missionary conscience of the People of God; to inform them about the needs of universal mission; and to encourage local churches to pray for and support one another with personnel and material aid" (TEE 13).

The last statement in the sentence quoted from the pastoral statement clearly points to the shift from a pre–Vatican II vision of mission as a movement from exclusively "mission-sending churches" to "mission countries" to a post–Vatican II relationship of mutuality among local churches in mission. People talk increasingly about this in terms of partnership and solidarity, a theme that is well developed in the U.S. bishops' 1997 statement, *Called to Global Solidarity*. For example, programs involving parish twinning and social justice awareness have great potential for promoting such mutuality in mission. Furthermore, the growing number of brief immersion experiences and short-term service-oriented volunteer opportunities outside one's own "world" often transform individuals with a whole new view of the why, who, and where of mission.

The Wedding Banquet as a Parable of Mission

For an image that captures the heart of this chapter, let us turn again to the words of Jesus, to the parable of the banquet as narrated by Matthew. "The reign of God may be likened to a king who gave a wedding banquet for his son. He dispatched his servants to summon the invited guests to the feast, but they refused to come" (Mt 22:2-3).

As we saw earlier, Jesus and the early church often used food and table fellowship to talk about the reign of God and mission. In this case, a feast has been prepared for a special occasion. The servants deliver the invitations to the invited guests, but they refuse to come. The king, who is anxious to have them at the table with him, doesn't give up but tries again. "A second time he sent other servants, saying: 'Tell those who are invited, See, I have my dinner prepared! My bullocks and corn-fed cattle are killed; everything is ready. Come to the feast'" (22:4).

Not only do those invited ignore the invitation, but some of them mistreat and even kill the messengers. The king punishes them for their actions. He turns his mind back to the waiting feast. "Then he said to his servants: 'The banquet is ready, but those who were invited were unfit to come. That is why you must go out into the byroads and invite to the wedding anyone you come upon'" (22:8-9).

The servants did as they were told, and the wedding hall was filled with guests. However, later the king encounters one person who is not properly dressed for a wedding feast. "'My friend,' he said, 'how is it you came in here not properly dressed?' The man had nothing to say" (22:12). The man is thrown out into the night. The expulsion evokes images of the Last Judgment and shows that actions must accompany faith (for a similar example see the parable of the two sons in Matthew 21:28-31).

In terms of motivation for mission, this parable illustrates the three models of mission of our century. In Jesus' description of the reign of God, our triune God in mission calls people to the wedding feast of his Son, the Messiah and Savior. The servants were prophets, apostles, and early disciples of Christ, and they continue to be those who are instruments of this mission of inviting people to the table. But not everyone accepts the invitation.

Those first invited represent the Jewish people who didn't believe in Christ. It is important to realize that the Gospels were written at a time of conflict between the early Christian community and the leaders of the Jewish people. Later in history, anti-Semitism has manifested itself in tragic ways, such as Nazism and the Holocaust. However, the church has expressed repentance for its part in such anti-Semitism, and the Second Vatican Council reaffirmed its positive relationship with Judaism (NA 4).

Today, the strong words for those who do not accept the invitation extend much broader. Furthermore, the initial warning toward the Jews also is pointedly extended to Christians with the additional story of the treatment of the person without the proper wedding garment. As we saw in Jesus' own ministry and in the Acts of the Apostles, the invitation is extended to sinners, tax-collectors, and lepers (those on the margins), and to the Gentiles, that is, to the nations. God's mission is not limited by human boundaries and categories. The feast is ready!

The image of the banquet points to the fullness of life that we are invited to share not only with God but also with others around the table. The hungers to be fed are both spiritual and physical. Mission is about salvation and liberation for body, mind, and soul. Sri Lankan theologian D. T. Niles described mission as "one beggar telling another beggar where to get food" (in Anderson 1994, 362). Why mission? All people are dependent on God and searching for nourishment. We are to share the good news that we have experienced and that we know, even if only partially. That good news is about God's mission of love, the reign of God, and Jesus Christ, the savior of all. The church, as the community of baptized Christians, is to be a sign and instrument of God's invitation to all. At the same time, Christians and the church in mission are challenged to be open to our own conversion by looking at the current state of our "wedding garment."

In reference to table fellowship, the Eucharist is the foretaste or sacrament of the banquet. Answering the questions of the why, who, and where of mission forms a straight line between who we are and what we do at home, in our church community, and in our world near and far. At each "table" we are to be "one beggar telling another beggar where to get food." Come to the banquet God has prepared for us!

In the next chapter we consider the what of mission.

Questions for Reflection

1. With which of the three models of mission do you most identify?
2. What one particular question related to mission challenges you, your parish, or the church in general?
3. Give an example or tell a story illustrating how the image of the banquet describes the why, who, and where of mission.

Suggestions for Further Reading

Official church documents:
Second Vatican Council, *Decree on the Missionary Activity of the Church (Ad Gentes)*, 1965.
Pope Paul VI, *On Evangelization in the Modern World (Evangelii Nuntiandi)*, 1975.
Pope John Paul II, *On the Permanent Validity of the Church's Missionary Mandate (Redemptoris Missio)*, 1990.
Congregation for the Doctrine of the Faith, *Doctrinal Note on Some Aspects of Evangelization*, 2007.

Bevans, Stephen B., and Roger P. Schroeder. *Constants in Context: A Theology of Mission for Today.* Maryknoll, NY: Orbis Books, 2004. Chapters 9–11. More detailed background on the three major Catholic mission documents/models in a broader, ecumenical context.
Burrows, William R., ed. *Redemption and Dialogue: Reading* Redemptoris Missio *and* Dialogue and Proclamation. Maryknoll, NY: Orbis Books, 1993. Complete texts with excellent commentaries and responses from various perspectives on two very important Catholic documents of the early 1990s.
Schreiter, Robert. "Changes in Roman Catholic Attitudes toward Proselytism and Mission." In *New Directions in Mission and Evangelization 2.* ed. James A. Scherer and Stephen B. Bevans, 113–25. Maryknoll, NY: Orbis Books, 1994. Excellent article that concisely traces the developing understanding of mission in the twentieth century through the stages of certainty, ferment, crisis, and rebirth.

7

A Single but Complex Reality

. . . .

The What of Mission

In Chapter 1 of this book we defined mission as *proclaiming, serving, and witnessing to God's reign of love, salvation, and justice.* How do we do this today? Chapter 6 dealt with the why, who, and where of mission. In this chapter we examine the what.

Pope John Paul II called mission "a single but complex reality" (RM 41). The particular form of mission depends greatly on the context or circumstances. Explicit proclamation of the gospel in public, for example, is not advisable in communist or Muslim countries. Missionaries and Catholics in Vietnam cannot publicly and explicitly proclaim or teach the gospel outside of church services. However, they are faithful to God's mission through their witness and conversation in their homes, their service to those recovering from addictions and suffering from AIDS, and their daily interactions with those of other faiths and Christian denominations. Even though their activity is restricted, they still fully participate in God's mission in their own context.

What forms of mission are relevant in the United States and Canada? First, we know there are many different situations. What shape does mission take in a western suburban parish? in the southern Bible Belt? in a southwestern Hispanic parish? in a traditional midwestern Catholic rural parish? in an eastern inner-city parish? What if one finds oneself living among or ministering to the "unchurched" in Appalachia? a youth group in Montreal? a retirement community in Florida? an ethnically mixed parish in Denver? an immigrant/refugee community on the U.S.-Mexican border? The question for this chapter, in other words, is this: how should Catholics participate in mission both within and beyond their local, cultural, ethnic, social, and national boundaries?

To form some sort of response, we will look at six components of the "single but complex reality" of mission that were briefly mentioned at the beginning of Chapter 4:

- witness and proclamation
- liturgy, prayer, and contemplation
- justice, peace, and the integrity of creation
- interreligious and secular dialogue
- inculturation
- reconciliation

In this chapter we draw parallels between these six forms or aspects of mission and the snapshots of Chapters 4 and 5, as well as other examples. These components have been present in some way throughout the history of Christianity. And they continue to be shaped by and to shape our response to our world and the understanding of mission today. It is important to note that these components of mission are distinct but not separate from one another. They are interconnected, and they are all important for full participation in God's mission today.

Witness and Proclamation

There is an essential link between witness and proclamation. As Pope Paul VI wrote, "The first means of evangelization is the witness of an authentically Christian life" (EN 41). How authentic are those who practice what they preach?

Witness as mission occurs on different levels. First of all, there are *individual Christians*. Some, like Mother Teresa of Calcutta, are widely known and live to a ripe old age. Countless others, from Blandina of the early church to Archbishop Oscar Romero of El Salvador, have witnessed through martyrdom. However, just as early Christians "gossiped the gospel," most witnessing is done by ordinary baptized Christians in their daily life at home, in their neighborhood, at work, and in social situations.

Second, witness happens *on the communal level* as a Christian community, a parish, and a diocese lives its life. Early Christian communities in cities around the Mediterranean reached out to help the sick and those in need. Parish communities ought to welcome and care for the migrant, the "outsider," and all those in need; they should have a positive impact on their neighborhood.

Third, witness moves beyond the local to the level of the *universal and institutional church*. The bishops of the United States have spoken out on issues of economy, peace, and racism, but the scandal of sexual abuse and the related coverups by several bishops has been a counter witness. Church-sponsored institutions like hospitals, schools, orphanages, and social-service centers witness to Christian values. Given the inevitability of the church as an institution falling short of its ideals, a willingness to confess to shortcomings without trying to shift blame can be a powerful witness in a society where inflating images and manipulating public relations have been made a science.

The fourth level is that of *common witness* to Jesus by Christian churches and denominations. Without denying the differences among them, Christians are called to avoid the scandal of presenting a divided Christ marked by rivalry and distrust. For example, there is a movement in the United States called Common Witness that enables and supports ecumenical collaboration for justice and service-oriented projects of mission. We recall the efforts of Cyril and Methodius, whom Pope John Paul II called the "authentic precursors of ecumenism."

To accompany witness, John Paul II spoke of *proclamation*— the explicit proclamation of Jesus Christ as Lord and Savior and his vision of the reign of God—as "the permanent priority of mission" (RM 44). In 1991 the Congregation for the Evangelization of Peoples and Pontifical Council for Interreligious Dialogue described proclamation this way: "It is an invitation to a commitment of faith in Jesus Christ and to entry through baptism into the community of believers which is the Church. This proclamation can be solemn and public, as for instance on the day of Pentecost (cf. Acts 2:5–41), or in a simple private conversation (cf. Acts 8:30–38)" (DP 10). Proclamation of the good news, like witness, has always been a key aspect of the church's mission.

However, sometimes proclamation has been and is still equated with a heavy-handed or manipulative approach, forcing the gospel down people's throats with the "sword and cross" approach in the Americas after 1492 or Christian missionaries' frequent hand-in-hand identification with colonialism in the nineteenth century. We remember how Bartolomé de Las Casas spoke against this approach very strongly. Today, we know that proclamation needs to be an invitation that respects the free choice of the listeners. In the words of John Paul II, "The Church proposes, she imposes nothing" (RM 39). So, a key question is *how* we proclaim. Proclamation must be linked with faithful Christian witness and respect for the "other." Maryknoll missionary Raymond Finch suggests that the best passage for mission today may be 1 Peter 3:15: "Should anyone ask you the reason for this hope of yours, be ever ready to reply, but speak gently and respectfully" (Finch 2000, 330). Proclamation begins with listening to and respecting the "other," as Jesus did with the Samaritan woman and Francis Xavier did with the Japanese. We know the popular saying *Jesus is the answer, but what is the question?* Only after listening to the deepest yearnings and hopes of others can we proclaim the good news in a way that is good news for them. Then the word of God (not the word of the Christian or the missionary) has the power and grace to call people to conversion and a new life.

Liturgy, Prayer, and Contemplation

We normally may not consider liturgy, prayer, and contemplation as acts of mission. However, centering our lives more and more on our God, who is missionary by nature, draws us into God's boundary-crossing mission.

As important and central to Christian life as liturgy is, it can't be an end in itself. The worshiping community needs to look beyond itself (see Schattauer 1999, 1–21). The dismissal prayer of the Eucharist, "Go in peace to love and serve the Lord," is sending the congregation in mission. Orthodox Christians describe this as the liturgy after the liturgy. How does what the Christian community experienced in the liturgy—listening to the word of God, forgiveness, reconciliation, and communion with God and one another—continue as people leave church?

A bishop tells the story of his experience with a group of grade-school children before their first communion. He asked them what the most important part of the Eucharist is. An eager little girl raised her hand, and when called upon, she pointed to the Exit sign. At first, the bishop was surprised by this response. However, when he asked her for an explanation, she said, "We are the body of Christ when we go out of church." He realized that she understood the meaning of the Eucharist very well.

Furthermore, mission is not just from "inside" (the church) to "outside," but also the reverse. Bringing the voices and concerns of the neighborhood and world into liturgy in various ways prevents the community from focusing too much on itself and opens its members to being attentive, nourished and challenged by God's movement in the wider world. Finally, the liturgy can be a means of mission for visitors, including those who never were or are no longer Christians. Such persons, who for some reason or another find themselves at a wedding, funeral, baptism, or a pilgrimage site, may be touched by a word, action, or gesture by a welcoming community celebrating a liturgy in a worthy fashion.

In 1927, Pope Pius XI proclaimed two saints patrons of missionary work—Francis Xavier and Thérèse of Lisieux. While Francis Xavier as an active missionary across Asia is a natural patron of mission, how can a nun who lived enclosed in a convent and who died at the age of twenty-four be a patron of mission? Thérèse touched the lives of many people after her death through her autobiography, *The Story of a Soul*. Her passion for mission is captured in her own words:

> I would want to preach the Gospel on all five continents and in the most remote islands. . . . I would want to be a missionary, not for a few years only but from the beginning of creation until the end of the ages.

By putting Francis and Thérèse side by side as patrons of mission, the pope emphasized that Christian living and mission consist of both activity and prayer.

In the British television series *Dr. Who,* the doctor would enter an enclosed telephone booth and then encounter the world in an amazing series of adventures. In a similar way, prayer and contemplation can draw us into seeing and encountering the world and others more and more from God's viewpoint. Silent contemplation within a cloister or religious community setting, regularly visiting the Blessed Sacrament in church, and prayer and meditation at home or in a hospital bed are all moments of entering such a "telephone booth" and aligning our lives with God's mission of love, salvation, and justice.

Pursuit of Justice, Peace, and the Integrity of Creation

The mission of God likewise calls the church to pursue work for a just and peaceful world and to care for God's gift of creation. As God's children, we are to live in right relationships with one another and with the world.

Caring for the poor and those in need has always been a part of the church's mission. Early Christian communities cared for the victims of plagues; East Syrian monasteries were places for medical care; beguines were involved in charitable works; Elizabeth of Hungary, Martin de Porres, Katherine Drexel, and Mother Teresa represent the hosts of Christians who reached out to the hungry and marginalized.

While this form of charitable work remains essential, a shift in the Catholic view of its mission began to occur with Pope Leo XIII's 1891 encyclical *The Condition of Labor (Rerum Novarum).* There Pope Leo laid the foundation for what has grown into an integrated body of Catholic social teaching. The church, he maintained, was called not only to take care of those in need but also to address the unjust social and economic structures and systems that put people in that situation. Proponents of this aspect of the mission of justice include historical figures like the Dominicans Montesinos and Las Casas in the Americas, Dorothy Day in the United States, and Bishop Oscar Romero in Central America. The U.S. bishops' statement *Economic Justice for*

All (1986) also illustrates this component of mission. Moving beyond speaking on behalf of others, the church needs to accompany the poor and victims in finding their own voice and choosing their own action. As the proverb states, It is not enough to give hungry people fish, but you have to teach them how to fish. Also, a commitment to justice has consequences for our lifestyle, political decisions, and solidarity with the poor. Finally, the church must practice justice internally to be a credible witness to others.

The devastation of war combined with the threat of nuclear and chemical weapons has cast a pall over our world. The tragic stories and experiences of soldiers and civilians of many affected nations, the event of 9/11, increased security measures, and the threat of terrorism make the search for peace a concern of all individuals and peoples. At Hiroshima, the site of the first hostile use of an atomic bomb, John Paul II said, "From now on it is only through a conscious choice and through a deliberate policy that humanity can survive" (1981).

Peace is not just the absence of violence. It requires ongoing positive and active choices. The church has the responsibility to challenge and support governments and other groups to make conscious choices and to follow deliberate policies for peace. This aspect of mission involves the church as a whole; examples include papal statements on World Peace Day (New Year's Day) and the U.S. bishops' 1983 pastoral letter *The Challenge of Peace: God's Promise and Our Response,* as well as the lobbying efforts by the conferences of men and women religious and Christian peace-and-justice groups. Individual Christians like Catherine of Siena, Francis of Assisi, Dorothy Day, and Martin Luther King Jr. have been prophetic figures of peacemaking and nonviolence. Such concerns likewise touch our families, neighborhoods, and parishes.

Concern for justice and peace within the human family extends to proper care for the rest of God's creation. Greed and injustice not only damage human beings but they also are the principal reasons for ecological damage. In 1971, Pope Paul VI called Christians to address the situation of the "ill-considered exploitation of nature" in *A Call to Action on the Eightieth Anniversary of* Rerum Novarum (no. 21), and in the same year the synod of bishops in Rome made the link between justice and preserving our natural resources and the biosphere itself (*Justice in the World*, chap. 1). In 1979, Pope John Paul II proclaimed Francis of Assisi the patron saint of ecology. Francis has been described as a "poet and nature mystic who discovered the transformation of the universe and the interrelatedness of all beings through a spiritual journey of conversion, penance and praise" (Nothwehr 2002, 99–100). In "The Canticle of Brother Sun," Francis's references to "Brother Sun" and "Sister Moon," "Brother Wind" and "Sister Water," "Brother Fire" and "Mother Earth" point to the unity and relationship of humanity with all of God's creation. Aligning ourselves with God's mission in terms of ecological responsibility requires us to think differently about human beings, earth's creatures, and the created universe itself. Mission includes witnessing to the goodness of God's creation and joining the rest of humanity in caring for it.

Interreligious and Secular Dialogue

In 1984, the Vatican Secretariat for Non-Christians' *The Attitude of the Church towards the Followers of Other Religions, Reflections and Orientations on Dialogue and Mission* insisted that "dialogue is . . . the norm and necessary manner of every form of Christian mission" (no. 29). This general principle and attitude is particularly important when encountering men and women of other faiths and those with no faith, as in a secular society. Meeting people of other religions is not limited to Asia, and meeting those with no faith is not limited to North America, Europe, Australia, and China. Dialogue is based on the belief that God's grace and love is present in all people. The Second Vatican Council never used the phrase "outside the church, no salvation." Rather, the council spoke of the possibility of salvation for all those of good will whether they believe in God or not (LG 16), and of other religious ways having "a ray of that truth which enlightens all" (NA 2). Therefore, Christians can learn something about God from others. On the one hand, we approach others with respect; at the same time, we remain true to our own Christian faith.

Official church documents point to four types of dialogue. We begin with the *dialogue of life*, as Christians interact in daily situations with people of other faiths or no faith. When we begin to meet and understand each other with real faces and personalities and not in generalizations, then much distrust and fear can be dissolved.

Second, in the *dialogue of action* Christians join with others to address common human concerns, such as peace, justice, and integrity. Violence and tension among religions and the events following 9/11 point to the urgent need for this dialogue.

Third, the *dialogue of religious experience* is an avenue for mutual enrichment by sharing the meaning and practice of prayer, meditation, and ritual. Although people of different religions may not be able to pray together, they can come together and pray in their own ways, as John Paul II did with other religious leaders at Assisi in 1986 and 2002.

Finally, there is the *dialogue of theological exchange*. This often takes place among experts discussing one another's doctrines and practices, such as Christians, Muslims, and Jews discussing the role of Jesus from their perspectives. However, such dialogue can also be done by ordinary Christians reading and discussing the sacred writings of other religions. Christians can dialogue with those with no belief about the spiritual yearnings in secular society expressed, for example, through literature, film, music, and technology.

The new perspective toward such interreligious and secular dialogue emerged explicitly since the Second Vatican Council, but similar moments or glimpses have occurred in the Christian tradition. We recall, for example, the attitude of Jesus toward the Roman centurion (Mt 8:10) and the Canaanite woman (Mt 15:28). To name a few others, East Syrian Christian monks interacted peacefully with Buddhists in seventh-century China; Francis of Assisi crossed the crusade battle lines to meet with the Muslim sultan; and Samuel Ajayi Crowther developed a working relationship with Muslims in West Africa. And we don't know the names of the many Christians who have been involved throughout history in the dialogue of life in rural and urban areas, in marketplaces and along trade routes, in coffee bars and over the Internet.

Biblical scholar Amos Yong analyzes the manner in which Jesus and the early church acted in relation to Jews and non-Jews, and to men and women in Jewish communities and social groups that were not thought well of by the establishment. His conclusion? The practice of Jesus and the early church was quite radical. The religious "other" is not simply an object for derision or conversion, nor is the "other" to be looked down upon. All others are *persons* that Christians should not hesitate to offer friendship to and accept friendship from (Yong 2008).

In dialogue with interreligious and secular partners, we listen to how God is already stirring in the hearts and traditions of the "other," and at the same time, we have the conviction that the fullness of truth and salvation was revealed and accomplished in Jesus Christ. Therefore, such dialogue does not replace or contradict the importance of proclamation mentioned above. We are either implicitly or explicitly proclaiming our Christian faith in dialogue, but we also have to remember the importance of how we proclaim. We are to listen respectfully to others speaking about their understanding of and search for truth, meaning, and God as *they* know them, and we are to do the same as *we* know them. As human beings, we do not know and experience the fullness of truth, but we Christians are to point and witness to the mystery, love, and fullness of God. Dialogue requires humility and openness as well as authenticity and integrity.

Inculturation

In novels and films the missionary is often depicted as blindly condemning the way of life of the local people. In James Michener's *Hawaii*, Barbara Kingsolver's *The Poisonwood Bible*, and Peter Matthiessen's *At Play in the Fields of the Lord*, one encounters arrogant missionaries who consider other cultures the work of the devil. While such characterizations were not always pushed to the extreme, many variations of what has been called the *tabula rasa* (blank slate) approach have been the norm for a long time. This was particularly true in missionary work since 1492, when the Christian faith became strongly identified with Western Christendom. At the same time, a more accommodating approach and more positive attitude toward culture were represented by missionaries such as Cyril and Methodius with Slavic peoples, Bartolomé de Las Casas in South America, Francis Xavier and other Jesuits in Asia, and Samuel Ajayi Crowther and Daniel Comboni in Africa. The Sacred Congregation for the Propagation of the Faith in 1659 reminded missionaries that it was not their task to "bring any pressure to bear on the peoples, to change their manners, customs, and uses, unless they are evidently contrary to religion and sound morals" (in Bevans and Schroeder 2004, 192).

The Second Vatican Council recovered this positive attitude toward culture. In encountering other peoples, the church "must implant itself . . . in the same way that Christ by his incarnation committed himself to the particular social and cultural circumstances" (AG 10). Recovering the image of Justin Martyr of the early church regarding the philosophy of his time, the council insisted that Christians "should be familiar with their national and religious traditions and uncover with gladness and respect those seeds of the Word which lie hidden among them" (AG 11). The local churches are to "borrow from the customs, traditions, wisdom, teaching, arts and sciences of their people everything which could be used to praise the glory of the Creator" (AG 22). During a famous address in Kampala (Uganda) several years after the council, Pope Paul VI proclaimed that "you may, and you must, have an African Christianity" (in Bevans and Schroeder 2004, 386). The word *inculturation* was introduced to capture this dynamic interaction between the gospel and church tradition, on the one hand, and the changing social and cultural context, on the other.

The images of the seeds and the weeds in the parables of Jesus, which we reviewed in Chapter 2, are very helpful in understanding inculturation as an essential aspect of mission. The seeds represent the word of God, which was planted among all peoples from the beginning of time (AG 11), but which always needs to be nurtured by the church today. That word of God is to continue to grow and bear fruit in the depths of who we are—individually, culturally, and socially. The weeds represent evil and all that is in opposition to the word of God. The gospel confronts the weeds found in every "garden" and calls for conversion. There is no single Christian culture. Seeing themselves as Christian nations, Europe and the United States often fell into the error of self-righteousness and the resulting blind condemnation of other peoples and their cultures. The missionaries thought that their own garden was only seeds and the garden of the other was only weeds. They were mistaken in both assumptions.

In *Christianity Rediscovered,* Spiritan missionary Vincent Donovan described how his Christian faith was enriched by the Maasai people of East Africa. Donovan later continued his missionary work of inculturation on a college campus and in a parish in the United States. The seeds of God's word are to be acknowledged, nurtured, and expressed in our own words, whether we are U.S. college students, Kenyan farmers, Brazilian health workers, or Chinese business persons. And everyone needs to do his or her share of weeding.

Reconciliation

The sixth and final component of mission is reconciliation. This is sometimes related to efforts of justice, peace, and the integrity of creation; however, increasing violence, terrorist threats, globalization (often eroding local values and excluding many from the benefits of the world economy), family breakdown, and the displacement and migration of many peoples are calling for a new response. The church as a reconciling community needs to join others in an appropriate way as the "hands and feet" of God in responding to this broken world.

This face of mission occurs on four different levels. They all depend, however, on the basic biblical horizon presented in 2 Corinthians 5:11–21, in which Paul is speaking of the human situation of being alienated from God by sin. In the background, however, is not sin as a mere transgression of law but as blindness to the nature of God as our creator and ourselves as able to find our salvation only in God. The Greek word the New Testament uses for "sin" is *hamartia*. It has the connotation of missing a target or being lost and unable to find the destination. In Paul's vision, humanity is lost and does not know the God who promises salvation and whose Spirit empowers us to follow the way of Jesus. Because we are lost, we flail about, hurt by the selfishness of others, hurting them in return, evil mounting up and undermining the social order. It is exactly this situation that Jesus seeks to make right, according to Paul, and he is struck down by those who do not want to respond to God's promises in him, for it is in opening oneself up to follow Jesus that God's justice will be secured for the world.

At another level, in this Pauline vision of the world, salvation is the acceptance of God's re-creating justice, but there is nothing we can do to deserve this graciousness. Rather, we accept it as a gift, and in accepting the gift, we are reconciled to God in Christ. Our vocation, accordingly, becomes that of making the way of Jesus known to all. In Paul's words:

> So if anyone is in Christ, there is a new creation: everything old has passed away; see, everything has become new! All this is from God, who reconciled us to himself through Christ, and has given us the ministry of reconciliation; that is, in Christ God was reconciling the world to himself, not counting their trespasses against them, and entrusting the message of reconciliation to us. So we are ambassadors for Christ, since God is making his appeal through us; we entreat you on behalf of Christ, be reconciled to God. For our sake he made him to be sin who knew no sin, so that in him we might become the righteousness of God. (2 Cor 5:17–21)

Practically, our vocation to be reconcilers is mediated, first of all, on a *personal* level; reconciliation is often necessary between spouses, between parent and child, and between victim and the perpetrator of violence and abuse. Those who have been victims of natural disasters or who have suffered through divorce and other broken relationships join the long list of those searching for God's healing.

Second, we can talk about *cultural* reconciliation for people whose culture has been denigrated or denied, such as Native Americans in the United States, aboriginals in Australia, and cultural minority groups in many parts of the world.

A third level is *political* reconciliation. This calls to mind the prophetic efforts of Nelson Mandela and Archbishop Desmond Tutu with the Truth and Reconciliation Commission in South Africa and similar efforts by others in Chile, Argentina, and Guatemala.

Fourth, there is a need for reconciliation *within the church* with those who often are marginalized, such as women, divorced

Catholics, certain cultural and racial groups, and those with a homosexual orientation. Most recently, the scandalous cases of sexual abuse by clergy and related coverups by some bishops has left many searching for wholeness and forgiveness.

Theologian Robert Schreiter has much practical experience of reconciliation. He also interprets reconciliation in Pauline terms, reminding us that at all four levels, it is God alone who can bring about reconciliation in people's hearts, but also that Christians are to be bridge-builders and mediators in the process (Schreiter 1992, 41–62). The church has a role and a responsibility to establish safe places and communities of reconciliation where the truth can be told and healing can be fostered in a trusting and prayerful environment. The Catholic Church's sacrament of reconciliation can be a powerful instrument of God's blessing and wholeness in this process. Reconciliation efforts are often painful, risky, and unsuccessful. However, Schreiter offers the following encouragement: "Churches should be trusting enough in the reconciling grace of God to admit their own failings and find ways of working toward reconciliation" (Schreiter 1998, 129).

Integrating the Single but Complex Reality of Mission

The six components above represent mission as "a single but complex reality," the way Pope John Paul II speaks of it (RM 41). In some ways we can distinguish among these various aspects, while in other ways they intersect and are interrelated. Witness and proclamation that are not reflected in prayer and liturgy, not concerned with justice, not aware of interreligious and secular realities, not inculturated so that they can be understood by the listeners, and/or not situated within a reconciled and reconciling community, are not complete. In certain times and places, one or the other component of mission will be more relevant and urgent. Reconciliation may take priority in the wake of Hurricane Katrina; interreligious understanding and dialogue may become more urgent after 9/11; justice and peace are necessary in the face of racial tension and poverty; proclamation is the necessary response to those hungry for the hope, love, and forgiveness of the explicit message of Jesus Christ; and witness often becomes the primary means of mission in communist and Muslim nations.

The three perspectives that together shape the why of mission—the loving Trinity, the reign of God, and Christ the Savior—provide the theological foundation for the form and what of mission described in this chapter.

The who and where of mission likewise apply here. While Christian individuals, communities, and organizations legitimately and quite appropriately may focus on one particular aspect of mission, we are all challenged to see the totality of that single but complex reality. It is in the subjects of mission—the actual followers of Jesus—that mission becomes real and the six components are integrated.

These six components are relevant for cross-cultural missionaries involved explicitly and intentionally in crossing boundaries, but also for all Christians called by their baptism into mission in their neighborhoods, families, schools, and work places. In the case of formal interreligious and secular dialogue, missionaries (ordained, religious, or lay) need specific and in-depth training. Still, ordinary Christians are increasingly engaged in the equally important dialogue of life and action with those of another or no religious belief among whom they work, study, or play. These specific aspects of mission, like mission itself, are not defined geographically. Interreligious dialogue is not limited to Asia; secular dialogue is not limited to Europe and North America; inculturation is not limited to Africa and Oceania; concern for justice and peace is not limited to Latin America and the Middle East.

What does mission mean for us on a practical and daily basis? While this question has been raised in the text and in a variety of ways in the questions at the end of each chapter, in the final chapter we delve explicitly into the spirituality and practice of mission, for it is here that the disciple grows in Christ and becomes his ambassador (2 Cor 5:20) in the highways and byways of the world.

Questions for Reflection

1. What idea in this chapter struck you as the most interesting?
2. Which of the six aspects of mission applies best to your situation?
3. What one particular question related to mission challenges you, your parish, or the church in general?

Suggestions for Further Reading

Bevans, Stephen B., and Roger P. Schroeder. *Constants in Context: A Theology of Mission for Today.* Maryknoll, NY: Orbis Books, 2004. Chapter 12. An in-depth theological description of the six components of mission with a focus on ecumenism.

Finch, Raymond. "Missionaries Today." *Origins* 30, no. 21 (2 November 2000), 327–32. A treatment of the five aspects of mission of Pope John Paul II, with a focus on the changing understanding of proclamation and catechesis.

Kirk, J. Andrew. *What Is Mission? Theological Explorations.* Minneapolis, MN: Fortress Press, 2000. Chapters 4–9. More detailed study of five of these six components of mission from an ecumenical Protestant perspective.

National Conference of Catholic Bishops. *The Challenge of Peace: God's Promise and Our Response.* Washington, DC: NCCB, 1983. Important U.S. bishops' statement on peace and mission.

National Conference of Catholic Bishops. *Economic Justice for All.* Washington, DC: NCCB, 1986. Important U.S. bishops' statement on justice and mission.

Schattauer, Thomas H., ed. *Inside Out: Worship in an Age of Mission.* Minneapolis, MN: Fortress Press, 1999. Collection of articles on liturgy and mission, with Schattauer's own article, "Liturgical Assembly as Locus of Mission," of particular relevance for parish life.

Schreiter, Robert. *The Ministry of Reconciliation: Spirituality and Strategies.* Maryknoll, NY: Orbis Books, 1998. Excellent resource on the component of reconciliation.

Yong, Amos. *Hospitality and the Other: Pentecost, Christian Practices, and the Neighbor.* Maryknoll, NY: Orbis Books, 2008. Careful biblical study, pointing to the importance and practicality of showing hospitality to those of other religions.

Zago, Archbishop Marcello. "Elements of the Mission *Ad Gentes.*" *Origins* 30, no. 21 (2 November 2000), 332–35. Excellent article by the former secretary of the Vatican Congregation for the Evangelization of Peoples on all the components of mission, with particular focus on harmonizing proclamation and dialogue.

8

The Mission-Driven Parish and Diocese

• •

The Spirituality and Practice—
the How—of Mission

Patrick Brennan is the pastor of Holy Family Parish in Inverness, Illinois, and the president of the National Center for Evangelization and Parish Renewal. In *The Mission Driven Parish* he presents practical suggestions for a parish that he believes is a church in mission both among its own members and in the world outside the community. The title and content of Brennan's work capture the intended outcome of this book: achieving a spirituality of mission.

Jesus described discipleship as building a house on rock, that is, on a solid foundation (Mt 7:24–27; Lk 6:47–49). Throughout the preceding pages we have laid a foundation for understanding and embracing the mission of God, the church, and our baptism. It is to be hoped that you have been relating the ideas in these chapters to your own life, parish, and diocese. In this final chapter we address more explicitly the question, What does this mean *for us* in the here and now? In other words, What is *our* next step in mission?

Rather than simply jumping into practical action, we need to remember the wisdom of Pope Pius XI in naming Francis Xavier and Thérèse of Lisieux together as the patron saints of mission. Therefore we too will weave together the spirituality and the practice of mission.

The Spirituality of Mission

The pre–Vatican II perception of mission spirituality was that grace flowed from God through the missionary or priest to the people. However, the Second Vatican Council recovered the understanding that God's grace has been and continues to be present in the world, in people of other churches and denominations, in other religions, and in other cultures. We have grown in our appreciation of God's grace coming to us through our daily experience. In the context of mission there is a multidirectional movement of grace through and from the people to the missionary, and among the people themselves. Sometimes this is referred to as mission in reverse or, in the words of Spiritan missionary Vincent Donovan, "Christianity rediscovered." The story of Peter and Cornelius (Acts 10:1–48) illustrates how God's Spirit was already stirring in the hearts of Cornelius and Peter before they met, and how that same Spirit continued to draw both men (along with Cornelius's household) to a moment of conversion.

Dialogue: Discovering How the Reign of God Is Already Present

Just as Peter and Cornelius listened to God's Spirit *already* present within their own hearts and within each other, so we are to have "a deep concern for the salvation of others and a profound respect for the ways they have already searched for and experienced God" (TEE 11). Furthermore, the church "not only gives of itself in service to the world and to the peoples of the world's cultures but learns from its involvement and expands its imagination of the depths of God's unfathomable riches" (Bevans and Schroeder 2004, 348). Personally, we need to develop a spirituality of humility and openness so we can do mission with an attitude and approach of humble listening. This translates into a mission practice, which is often called dialogue. In Chapter 7 we referred to dialogue with interreligious and secular partners as one of the components of mission. Here we are broadening the scope of the term to also describe mission in general.

The U.S. bishops took the following statement from the Vatican Secretariat for Non-Christians' *The Attitude of the Church towards the Followers of Other Religions, Reflections and Orientations on Dialogue and Mission*, making it their own:

> Dialogue is . . . the norm and necessary manner of every form of Christian mission, as well as of every aspect of it, whether one speaks of simple presence and witness, service or direct proclamation. Any sense of mission not permeated by such a dialogical spirit would go against the demands of true humanity and against the teachings of the Gospel. (TEE 40)

Developing the spirituality and skills to practice dialogue both humbly and authentically continues to challenge us.

Prophecy: Discerning How the Reign of God Is Not Yet Present

While seeing mission as dialogue is an important corrective to the predominant mission spirituality and practice prior to the council, it is just one, albeit an essential, side of the coin. As early in history as Genesis, humanity and the world are in need of redemption and reconciliation. Throughout the Hebrew scriptures the prophets reminded the Israelites of God's love and presence, but they also challenged their faithlessness to God and their mistreatment of orphans and widows. Jesus affirmed God's love for humanity, but his prophetic words and action challenged people to be attentive to those on the edge of society, to rethink their understanding of the Law, and to die to the old ways and be reborn in the new. Jesus Christ, as the prophetic Word of God, also pointed to how the reign of God was *not yet present*. Both Peter and Cornelius, the one being sent and the one receiving, were challenged by that same prophetic word of God. We too are called to conversion and transformation. One phrase that attempts to capture this two-sided spirituality and practice of mission is *prophetic dialogue*.

Prophetic Dialogue:
Discerning the Already and the Not Yet

Speaking as a Christian minority, the Roman Catholic bishops of Asia were among the first to speak of mission as dialogue, more specifically, as a threefold dialogue with the poor, with culture, and with other religions. But they also articulated that, while maintaining a stance of compassion, appreciation, and respect, mission needs to be *prophetic* in speaking out against that which puts and keeps the poor in that state, in pointing out those aspects of culture that are contrary to the reign of God, and in maintaining that Jesus is the way, the truth, and the life (Jn 14:6).

The spirituality and practice of mission go hand in hand. We need to develop a spiritual attentiveness and a discerning spirit for acknowledging and affirming God's reign and the seeds of the word of God and for naming and uprooting those weeds that are contrary to the reign of God. A key aspect of this spiritual and practical process is that it is done within a broader community, both a church community and social/cultural community. Whether engaging others as an "insider" or an "outsider" to their cultural, religious, economic, national, or generational world, the agent of mission needs to trust that the "other" has God's Spirit, along with the accompanying ability and responsibility to distinguish between seeds and weeds, and the freedom and grace to make the choice to respond. We know how difficult this can be within our own family and parish, and what additional challenges occur when we cross those boundaries.

The practice of this sort of mission spirituality can be described as respectfully and humbly entering the "garden" or world of meaning of the "other." By allowing others to show us their garden (in their own way and at their own pace), perhaps eventually we can accompany them as *they* distinguish between the seeds and the weeds in their garden, as we should in ours (Schroeder 2000). Entering someone else's garden can occur when visiting a young divorced Catholic in a hospital, collaborating with black Muslims in inner-city Newark on an issue of justice, sponsoring or teaching an RCIA candidate, or working with the poor in another country. It is important to note that these examples are representative of the various components of mission presented in the last chapter. In other words, the spirituality of prophetic dialogue has an impact on every act and aspect of mission practice, including ministry and leadership styles and the use of money and material resources. Whatever we do, we need humbly to acknowledge, nurture, and engage with the way God is already stirring in the "other" and in us. At the same time we need to be open and attentive to God's word, which is calling the other and us to up-root the weeds and be transformed.

But what does this mean practically *for us*?

Practice of Mission

In 1997 the U.S. bishops issued a statement entitled *Called to Global Solidarity: International Challenges for U.S. Parishes.* The following year they published a booklet with the document and extensive handouts, resources, and practical suggestions for action. Many dioceses have found this very helpful in moving from basic principles to parish ministries and activities. We will use this document to address mission from a parish perspective, and then we will situate the practice of mission within a broader framework.

Called to Global Solidarity is founded upon the universal (catholic) nature and social teachings of the church. As the bishops say, "A parish reaching beyond its own members and beyond national boundaries is a truly 'catholic' parish. An important role for the parish is to challenge and encourage every believer to greater global solidarity" (CGS 1 [page numbers in the text refer to the 1998 booklet]). Solidarity implies seeing *all* people as brothers and sisters within God's human family and being transformed in such a way that we act "on behalf of the one human family, calling us to help overcome the divisions in our world" (CGS 4). In a similar vein, Pope John Paul II had stated in 1999: "For the particular Churches of the American continent, [solidarity] is the source of a commitment to reciprocal solidarity and the sharing of the spiritual gifts and material goods with which God has blessed them" (EA 52). How can Catholics in the United States respond to this call to solidarity and mission?

Catholic Relief Services, through its Lenten Operation Rice Bowl program with the accompanying Home Calendar Guide, invites Catholic individuals and families to pray and fast "in solidarity with the hungry around the world," to learn more about the real life situation of the poor, and to assist them financially around the world and within the United States. The Society for the Propagation of the Faith, through such programs as World Mission Sunday and the Missionary Cooperation Plan, provides a means for Catholics to be in solidarity with missionary activity and with local churches around the world. The Holy Childhood Association provides materials and programs to develop children's understanding of mission and their sense of solidarity with the broader human family, especially with other children. The church's Migration and Refugee Services works through over a hundred dioceses to assist and integrate immigrants, refugees, and other displaced peoples within U.S. society and within the Catholic Church. The Committee on World Mission of the U.S. bishops coordinates and animates overseas mission efforts on behalf of the U.S. church, as spelled out in TEE. The U.S. Catholic Mission Association unites, supports, and collaborates with religious, lay, and diocesan mission-sending agencies working both within and outside the country. The Catholic Network of Volunteer Services joins more than two hundred faith-based lay programs committed to domestic and/or overseas mission service. These organizations, along with many others, provide means for Catholics, nationally and locally, to reach beyond their own margins in mission.

The parish-twinning program is an excellent opportunity for promoting mutuality and solidarity. Over seventeen hundred U.S. parishes have connections with Catholic communities and parishes in Central and South America. The U.S. bishops have endorsed this program: "We welcome 'twinning' relationships and encourage the development of these relationships in ways that avoid dependency and paternalism. These bridges of faith offer as much to U.S. parishes as their partners. We are evangelized and changed as we help other communities of faith" (CGS 10). Programs for partnering parishes within the United States have similar potential. In addition, many Catholics who participate in the increasing number of opportunities for short-term immersion and/or service-oriented programs have a profound experience of going beyond their own boundaries and of being transformed into Christians committed to mission and service in a variety of ways. In such activities, as with any of those mentioned above, people are constantly challenged to develop and maintain a relationship of mutuality and respect, not dependency and paternalism. Diocesan mission offices have the challenging responsibility for promoting mission cooperation through the Pontifical Mission Societies as well as other programs in order to create, ideally, a mission-driven diocese.

What does this mean on a parish level? Locally initiated opportunities include parish committees focused on human concerns, social justice, sanctity of all life, and/or evangelization. Liturgy and catechesis provide opportunities for remembering Christian witnesses and martyrs from other parts of the world and for developing solidarity with the needs and issues of others. Many parishes have developed ecumenical and interfaith bridges to address common issues on the local, national, and international levels. Catholic individuals, families, and parishes respond to local needs for food, shelter, and community. The growing presence of Catholics—lay, religious, and priests—from other areas in the United States brings the global issues close to home and provides wonderful opportunities for developing mutual relationships beyond one's own margins. "A parish's 'catholicity' is illustrated in its willingness to go beyond its own boundaries to extend the Gospel, serve those in need, and work for global justice and peace. This is not a work for a few agencies or one parish committee, but for every believer and every local community of faith" (CGS 5). We remember here the essential link among baptism, church, and mission—as lived by the early Christian communities and as lifted up by the Second Vatican Council.

Drawing upon the organizations and programs mentioned above, as well as others, over 80 percent of the 1998 edition of the CGS booklet is devoted to presenting resources and practical suggestions for doing mission in the parish. These provide a framework (CGS 8–11), suggestions for action, and parish examples (CGS 13–23) in the areas of (1) prayer, worship, and preaching, (2) education and formation, (3) work, family, and citizenship, (4) stewardship, (5) outreach and charity, and (6) advocacy and political responsibility. CGS includes suggestions for getting started and for making an initial assessment in these six areas. (Appendix 1 of this book contains a sample parish-assessment tool that was adapted from the CGS material for the Archdiocese of Cincinnati.) The last section of CGS comprises an extensive and valuable collection of handouts and resources (CGS 25–42): discussion questions, suggestions for individuals and families, calendar information, fact sheets, bulletin quotes, print and video resources, contact information for additional organizations and programs, and material available from the U.S. bishops. The amount of material may appear overwhelming, but it is offered to suggest what the next step may be. CGS is an excellent resource for the practice of mission around the theme of solidarity for a parish. A number of mission office directors have also found *Sharing Gifts in the Global Family of Faith* by Mennonites Pakisa Tshimika and Tim Lind to be a very helpful resource on the diocesan level.

The United States Conference of Catholic Bishops published a statement for World Mission Sunday in 2005 entitled *Teaching the Spirit of Mission* Ad Gentes: *Continuing Pentecost Today.* The document affirms the importance of being in solidarity with missionary efforts around the world through mission education in the family and parish, the celebration of Mission Sunday, parish-twinning relationships, and emphasis of world mission in Catholic schools and seminaries. (For supplemental resources with practical suggestions for bishops, rectors, and university/seminary professors, priests and deacons, parents, and DREs/catechists/teachers, select the "best practices" tab on the Committee on World Missions section of the USCCB website. For a list of additional website sources on mission, see Appendix 2 of this book.)

Once Again, Mission as a Single but Complex Reality

We can connect with the broader understanding of the what of mission by briefly pointing to the six components of the "single, but complex reality" (RM 41) of mission within CGS. *Proclamation* is most evident in the goals and activities of the Sacred Congregation for the Propagation of the Faith and the Holy Childhood Association and through education, formation, and preaching on the parish level. *Witness* is implied throughout the entire document. *Liturgy and prayer* are featured as the essential means for "anchoring" solidarity and mission (CGS 8, 15–16). The component of *justice and peace* is very prominent in this document, represented, for example, by Operation Rice Bowl and other programs of Catholic Relief Services and parish human-concerns committees. The contribution of *interreligious and secular dialogue* in this context falls under the dialogue of action—working with interfaith groups and secular organizations and networks. While *inculturation* is not mentioned explicitly, the entire intent of the bishops' statement is that the word of God take deeper root in the daily lives of individuals and parishes, so that they in turn participate in the transformation of the culture and society of an area, a nation, and the world. Finally, God's call to *reconciliation* is the underlying motivation for responding to problems caused by globalization, for making efforts to overcome divisions, and for striving for solidarity.

These components of mission overlap in practice, as they do in theory. One can *distinguish* but not *separate* the parts of the whole. It is crucial that all elements are in some way present in any document or action plan intending to represent a comprehensive approach to mission. The absence of a concern for justice, proclamation, liturgy, or inculturation points to a deficiency. At the same time, every church document, organization, and parish or diocesan plan by necessity has a certain lens or starting point. For example, CGS is heavily shaped by issues of justice, peace, and reconciliation, while TEE focuses on "the proclamation of the gospel to peoples outside the United States" (TEE 3). TEE, then, focuses on mission outside the United States, and CGS focuses on the task of mission within the country, but each document acknowledges and supports the practice of mission in both contexts. It is good to look at these documents together, as we did in Chapter 6 with the three major documents of the universal church (AG, EN, and RM). While they have different starting points and purposes, both situate mission within that "single but complex reality."

This perspective has practical applications. On the diocesan level different individuals and/or offices are assigned responsibility for one or more organizations or ministries, such as Propagation of the Faith, Holy Childhood, Catholic Relief Services, Ethnic Ministries, Social Justice, Religious Education, and Migration and Refugee Services. Tension can arise due to conflicting goals, different models of mission (theology), competitive fundraising, and/or narrow vision. As the different components of mission (with a variety of combinations) are to be woven together into a single but complex reality, diocesan personnel and ministers are challenged to see themselves and others as different parts of the one body, the body of Christ (see 1 Cor 12:12–31), with the one mission of Christ. Similar dynamics, challenges, and opportunities occur on the parish level as well. "There are different gifts but the same Spirit; there are different ministries but the same Lord; there are different works but the same God who accomplishes all of them in everyone. To each person the manifestation of the Spirit is given for the common good" (1 Cor 12:4–7).

Let us return to the national level. For a number of years U.S. mission agencies and organizations often felt as if they were going in different directions. An important shift was signaled in 2000 as the church used the moment of entering the new millennium to come together to reflect upon its responsibility for and experience of mission. A national mission conference held in Chicago was jointly sponsored by the various constituencies of the U.S. Catholic Church involved in both overseas and domestic mission: Catholic Network of Volunteer Services (laity in mission), Conference of Major Superiors of Men, Leadership Conference of Women Religious, National Conference of Catholic Bishops—Committee of World Mission, Pontifical Mission Societies, and the United States Catholic Mission Association. Over 650 persons participated in Mission Congress 2000, described in the winter 2000 issue of *Mission Trends* as "a motivational and inspirational event that raised up important elements of mission to be considered in the future design of mission institutes, diocesan and parish mission endeavors, and programs engaging laity in mission and volunteer service. . . . The Congress focused on contemporary ways in which the Catholic Church experiences and practices mission." The next national mission congress in 2005 in Tucson had additional sponsorship from the bishops' committee on home mission and the Secretariat for the Church in Latin America. These two events were opportunities for different parts of the U.S. Catholic Church to look at mission together as a "single but complex reality."

Although we have placed our accent on the statements of the Vatican Council, the popes, and the American bishops in this book, it is important to recall also that communities of priests, lay people, brothers, and sisters are one of the primary ways in which the church acts in mission. The website of the United States Catholic Mission Association is a good place to start looking for the self-descriptions of communities such as the Maryknoll Fathers and Brothers, various male and female branches of the Franciscan orders, lay missionary organizations, and many other groups active in world mission. The addresses and websites to which you will be directed from the USCMA are also full of resources, such as books, DVDs, other audiovisual materials, and information on Catholic mission worldwide.

Table Fellowship as the Goal of Mission in Its Fullness

The theme of table fellowship and mission has been one of the threads through this book. In Chapter 1 we were invited to link Jesus, as the bread of life, with our daily life (table at home), our Christian faith (the eucharistic table), and our world (table of the "other"). Chapters 2 and 3 provided detailed descriptions of the significance of table fellowship in the mission of Jesus and of the early church (particularly in the Peter and Cornelius story and during the Council of Jerusalem). In later chapters we traced the successes and failures of the church in its efforts to be faithful to this mission of Jesus. The table-fellowship theme is reflected in Chapter 6 through Jesus' use of the wedding-banquet image. While not spelled out explicitly in Chapters 7 and 8, one can easily see how the current situation and understanding of the church is focused on linking daily life, Christian faith, and our world—both in spirituality and in practice.

In Chapter 1 we mentioned the centrality of this table imagery in the 2002 U.S. bishops' statement *A Place at the Table*, which addressed the particular issue and reality of poverty. This theme is likewise present in the two major U.S. bishops' documents on mission that were primary sources for us. TEE begins its development of this topic in its third section, "A Mission Spirituality," with the story of the multiplication of the loaves. While the disciples felt overwhelmed and inadequate facing the crowds and the demands of mission, Jesus showed them how they were to give of themselves to others. In the same way, "we must be willing to share Christ's nourishment with other parishes and dioceses . . . [and] be willing to bring this nourishment to other lands and gather all nations, all peoples, at the table of the Lord" (TEE 53). Furthermore, this is to be done in the spirit of hospitality and mutuality: "Like the disciples, we must be prepared to share what we have and to accept what others offer us" (TEE 54). The bishops draw an immediate connection between the Eucharist (TEE 55) and the daily cost of discipleship (TEE 56), and this is summarized in the following way: "The Eucharist nourishes our mission spirituality and strengthens our commitment to give of ourselves and our resources to the development of the diocesan and universal Church as a people aware of our responsibility for, and interdependence with, all peoples of the earth" (TEE 58). What a wonderful statement capturing the symbol of table fellowship and mission and introducing the idea of solidarity, which is developed in the next document.

CGS insists that the work of solidarity (and mission) with all people both at home and abroad is the responsibility of "every believer and every local community of faith" (CGS 5). This needs to be reflected in prayer and particularly "in the eucharist the Church prays for the peace of the world and the growth of the Church in love, and it advances these gifts" (CGS 3). The resource materials elaborate on the role of prayer, worship, and preaching for anchoring solidarity and provide many practical suggestions for achieving this (CGS 15–16). "In our parishes, the eucharist represents a central setting for discovering and expressing our commitment to our brothers and sisters throughout the world. Gathered around the altar, we are reminded of our connection to all of God's people through the mystical body of Christ" (CGS 8). This expression of table fellowship and mission is very challenging and crucial for both the spirituality and practice of mission.

Summing Up:
What *Is* the Mission of the Church?

In Chapters 2 and 3 we laid the foundation with the "big picture" of the mysterious, loving, and saving mission and plan of

God and the emergence of the church, particularly as told in the Acts of the Apostles. The encounters of Jesus with the Samaritan woman and Peter with Cornelius (and his household) were key stories representing this ongoing movement of God's Spirit in mission in our world. We then looked at snapshots of mission practice through history in Chapters 4 and 5. This provided an opportunity for a more complete understanding and appreciation of the single but complex reality of our Christian tradition, with its weaknesses and strengths. In the final three chapters we situated ourselves in our current context. We drew upon church documents and other resources as we reflected on the experience of mission and the reality of our world. We probed the questions of the why, who, where (Chapter 6), what (Chapter 7), and how (Chapter 8) of mission today.

We have seen how the Spirit is both challenging (prophetic) and affirming (dialogue) in the biblical story of Peter and Cornelius, and later in the stories of Blandina and Alopen, Cyril and Methodius, Francis of Assisi, the beguines, Francis Xavier, Thérèse of Lisieux, Samuel Ajayi Crowther, Daniel Comboni, Dorothy Day, Mother Teresa, and countless others. The one Spirit moves all to participate creatively in God's mission in their own time and place.

The Spirit challenges us to do the same. While this chapter discusses practical applications, I hope it also encourages us to look at our own situation and to reflect upon our own response. That, at least, was the intention. The response to mission should affect our minds, hearts, and actions.

May we as church respond humbly and prophetically to the challenges and opportunities of mission today.

Questions for Reflection

1. What three things can you do in your home, parish, or diocese as your "next step" in mission?
2. Describe the link between spirituality and practice of mission.
3. What image, person, or story of mission from this book has been most inspiring for you?

Suggestions for Further Reading

Brennan, Patrick. *The Mission Driven Parish*. Maryknoll, NY: Orbis Books, 2007. Theological and social science foundations and practical advice for pastors and parishes.

George, Sherron Kay. *Called as Partners in Christ's Service: The Practice of God's Mission*. Louisville, KY: Geneva Press, 2004. Very readable text addresses particularly parish-twinning relationships.

Gittins, Anthony. *Ministry at the Margins: Strategy and Spirituality for Mission*. Maryknoll, NY: Orbis Books, 2002. Spiritual and practical insights on cross-cultural mission and ministry, at home and abroad.

National Conference of Catholic Bishops. *Called to Global Solidarity: International Challenges for U.S. Parishes. A Statement of the National Conference of Catholic Bishops with Parish Resources*. Washington, DC: USCC, 1998. Major U.S. bishops' mission document and excellent practical resources and suggestions.

National Conference of Catholic Bishops. *To the Ends of the Earth: A Pastoral Statement on World Mission*. Washington, DC: USCC, 1986. Paragraphs 51–75. "A Mission Spirituality" and "Conclusion" from a key U.S. mission document.

Schroeder, Roger. "Entering Someone Else's Garden: Cross-Cultural Mission/Ministry." In *The Healing Circle*, ed. Stephen Bevans, Eleanor Doidge, and Robert Schreiter, 147–61. Chicago: CCGM Publications, 2000. Description of basic dynamics in passing over into another world view, whether near or far away.

Tshimika, Pakisa K., and Tim Lind. *Sharing Gifts in the Global Family of Faith: One Church's Experiment*. Intercourse, PA: Good Books, 2003. Reflections by Mennonites on mission as an exchange of gifts among churches.

Appendix 1:
A Sample Parish Assessment Tool

Catholic Mission and Global Solidarity Parish Assessment Tool

From the Mission Office, Archdiocese of Cincinnati,
March 2006
(513) 421–3131   www.catholiccincinnati.org/mission

General

- What do we know about our parish's connection to our church's world mission effort and to international issues? Where does the call to promote Catholic mission efforts and global solidarity fit into the life of our parish? Is Jesus' call to evangelization, mission, and solidarity central and a consistent commitment for our entire community of faith or a task left to a few committee members or individuals?

- Do parishioners understand what the Catholic Social Teaching *solidarity* means and the post Vatican II "humble, mutual, solidarity model" of mission? Has our parish helped them think about what it would mean to be in solidarity around the world?

- Does our parish already have or could it consider establishing a mutually enhancing and spiritually rewarding "twinning" relationship with another parish or organization in a different culture in the U.S. or overseas? (see www.catholiccincinnati.org/mission)

- Are there parishioners from different parts of the world or who have lived in other cultures who could be helpful in sharing their experiences and developing a project?

- Is there an immigrant or refugee community in the area with which our parish could connect and dialogue? How could they evangelize and mission to us? Join our church?

- How many lay or religious missionaries are from our parish? Do we know them and support them? Do our parishioners know of the 200 Catholic lay missionary, volunteer organizations in the U.S. or overseas that could use their skills or resources, short or long term? (Visit www.CNVS.org for Catholic Network of Volunteer Service)

- How is our parish working with our archdiocesan Mission Offices? How could our parishioners and staff make better use of their teacher in-service programs, educational resources, videos, websites, advice on mission/immersion trips, and other contacts?

Anchoring Mission and Solidarity: Prayer, Worship, and Preaching

- How is our concern for our sisters and brothers around the world and the 1,150 mission dioceses reflected in our parish's prayer, worship, and preaching? Do we truly recognize Jesus' face in the poor and oppressed? What could they teach us about faith in God?

- Is mission and global solidarity appropriately and regularly woven into the homilies?

- Are they reflected in general intercessions, special prayer services, and the prayers that open parish meetings?

Teaching Mission and Solidarity: Education and Formation

- Do our religious education and sacramental preparation programs include opportunities to study about Jesus' mission mandate, the missionary work of St. Paul, the apostles and early church? Do they know of the co-patrons of our church's missionary work, Fr. Francis Xavier and St. Thérèse of Lisieux? Do they know of our more recent missionary martyrs like Sr. Dorothy Stang of our archdiocese and Jean Donavan of Cleveland?

- How is our church's current mission efforts in the U.S. (like Glenmary) and overseas (like Maryknoll) and teaching on international justice and peace taught in our parish's education programs? Are they given opportunities to act on this teaching?

- Have our adults or children been able to dialogue with current or recently returned missionaries? Do we hold adult education programs on church teaching and/or international policy issues? Do we know how the Mission Office could help?

- How could our parish organize a visit to one of archdiocesan missionaries in the U.S. or overseas? Might we be enriched by meeting more "faces" of God by visiting other faith communities? What guide booklet does the Mission Office offer on safety and liability?

Living Solidarity: Work, Family, and Citizenship

- How does our parish encourage individuals and families to reflect a commitment to short or long term missionary, volunteer service as well international justice and peace in their family, work, and public lives?

- Are they given information about the impact of their consumer choices on workers around the world? Do we acknowledge and affirm those who work in the area of international concerns (e.g., missionary programs, Foreign Service, or Peace Corps)?

- Are parishioners encouraged to participate in political life in ways that promote international justice and peace? Do the needs of the poorest have the highest priority?

Investing in Mission and Solidarity: Stewardship, Outreach and Charity

- How are parish collections for Catholic missionary organizations and other international programs handled? Are they seriously explained and promoted?

- Do parishioners know the purpose of World Mission Sunday in late October and the work of the Pontifical Society For the Propagation of the Faith that supports 1,150 mission dioceses? How could the Mission Co-op Plan (visiting missioners) be improved?

- Do our children know how to participate in the Pontifical Holy Childhood Association?

- Do preachers link the Gospel to these collections? Are they seen as opportunities to share Catholic teaching on international concerns?

Promoting Solidarity: Advocacy and Political Responsibility

- What information and opportunities are given to parishioners regarding international peace and justice issues? Are they aware of missionary organizations' view points?

- Does our parish participate in a legislative network? Are "action alerts" on international issues shared through the bulletin or through a telephone tree or mailing list?

Appendix 2:
Resources and Contact Information

Catholic Network of Volunteer
   Services
www.cnvs.org
301–270–0900

Catholic Relief Services
www.crs.org
866–608–5978

Center of Concern
www.coc.org
202–635–2757

Columban Fathers' Mission
   Education Office
www.columban.org/missioned
877–299–1920 (toll free)

Conference of Major Superiors
   of Men's Institutes
www.cmsm.org
301–588–4030

From Mission to Mission
www.missiontomission.org
720–494–7211

The Holy Childhood Association
www.holychildhoodusa.org
202–775–8637

Jesuit Conference Office of Social
   and International Ministries
www.jesuit.org
202–462–0400

JustFaith Ministries
www.justfaith.org
502–429–0865

Leadership Conference of
   Women Religious
www.lcwr.org
301–588–4955

Maryknoll World Productions
www.maryknollmall.org
800–227–8523

Mexican American Cultural
   Center
www.maccsa.org
210–732–2156

National Council of Catholic
   Women
www.nccw.org
800–506–9407

Pax Christi USA
www.paxchristiusa.org
814–453–4955

Pontifical Mission Societies
www.worldmissions
  -catholicchurch.org
212–563–8700

USCCB Committee on World
  Mission
www.usccb.org/wm
202–541–3000

United States Catholic
  Conference of Bishops
www.usccb.org
800–235–8722

US Catholic Mission Association
www.uscatholicmission.org
www.mission-education.org
202–832–3112

Vatican
www.vatican.va

Select Diocesan or Regional Mission Office Websites

www.catholiccincinnati.org/mission (Cincinnati, OH)

www.diogh.org/socialjustice_missions (Galveston-Houston, TX)

www.archmil.org/resources/userfiles/worldmis/Worldlibrary2
.htm (Milwaukee, WI)

www.stclouddiocese.org/mission (Saint Cloud, MN)

www.catholicmissionmn.org/center_for_mission/ (St. Paul-Minneapolis, MN)

www.catholicmissionmn.org/center_for_mission/global_
solidarity/htm (St. Paul-Minneapolis, MN)

www.texasmissioncouncil.org (Texas Mission Council)

Bibliography / Reference List

Official Catholic Church Documents Related to Mission after 1960 (in chronological order)

Vatican Council II. *Lumen Gentium (Dogmatic Constitution on the Church)*. 21 November 1964.

Vatican Council II. *Nostra Aetate (Declaration on the Relation of the Church to Non-Christian Religions)*. 28 October 1965.

Vatican Council II. *Dignitatis Humanae (Declaration on Religious Liberty)*. 7 December 1965.

Vatican Council II. *Ad Gentes (Decree on the Missionary Activity of the Church)*. 7 December 1965.

Vatican Council II. *Gaudium et Spes (Pastoral Constitution on the Church in the Modern World)*. 7 December 1965.

Pope Paul VI. *Octogesima Adveniens (A Call to Action on the Eightieth Anniversary of* Rerum Novarum*)*. Apostolic letter. 14 May 1971.

Synod of Bishops. *Justice in the World*. 30 November 1971.

Pope Paul VI. *Evangelii Nuntiandi (On Evangelization in the Modern World)*. Apostolic exhortation. 8 December 1975.

National Conference of Catholic Bishops. *The Challenge of Peace: God's Promise and Our Response*. Washington, DC. 1983.

Secretariat for Non-Christians. *The Attitude of the Church towards the Followers of Other Religions, Reflections and Orientations on Dialogue and Mission*. 1984.

John Paul II. *Slavorum Apostoli (Apostles of the Slavs)*. Encyclical letter. 2 June 1985.

National Conference of Catholic Bishops. *Economic Justice for All*. Washington, DC. 13 November 1986.

National Conference of Catholic Bishops. *To the Ends of the Earth: A Pastoral Statement on World Mission*. Washington, DC. 12 November 1986.

John Paul II. *Redemptoris Missio (On the Permanent Validity of the Church's Missionary Mandate)*. Encyclical letter. 7 December 1990.

Congregation for the Evangelization of Peoples and Pontifical Council for Interreligious Dialogue. *Dialogue and Proclamation*, 1991.

United States Catholic Conference. *Catechism of the Catholic Church*. Mahwah, NJ: Paulist Press, 1994.

United States Conference of Catholic Bishops. *Called to Global Solidarity: International Challenges for U.S. Parishes.* Washington, DC. 12 November 1997.

John Paul II. *Ecclesia in America (The Church in America)*. Postsynodal apostolic exhortation. 22 January 1999.

National Conference of Catholic Bishops. *A Place at the Table*. Washington, DC. 13 November 2002.

National Conference of Catholic Bishops. *Teaching the Spirit of Mission* Ad Gentes: *Continuing Pentecost Today*. June 2005.

Congregation for the Doctrine of the Faith. *Doctrinal Note on Some Aspects of Evangelization*. 3 December 2007.

Basic Resources on Mission and for Mission Education

Anderson, Gerald H., et al., ed. 1994. *Mission Legacies: Biographical Studies of Leaders of the Modern Missionary Movement*. Maryknoll, NY: Orbis Books.

Bevans, Stephen B., and Roger P. Schroeder. 2003. "Keeping Current: The New Church History." *New Theology Review* 16, no. 4: 79–81.

———. 2004. *Constants in Context: A Theology of Mission for Today*. Maryknoll, NY: Orbis Books.

Bosch, David J. 1991. *Transforming Mission: Paradigm Shifts in Theology of Mission*. Maryknoll, NY: Orbis Books.

———. 1994. "The Vulnerability of Mission." In *New Directions in Mission and Evangelization 2*, ed. James A. Scherer and Stephen B. Bevans, 73–86. Maryknoll, NY: Orbis Books.

Brennan, Patrick. 2007. *The Mission Driven Parish*. Maryknoll, NY: Orbis Books.

Devlin, Dennis. 1984. "Feminine Lay Piety in the High Middle Ages: The Beguines." In *Medieval Religious Women: Distant Echoes*,

Cistercian Studies Series 71, ed. Lillian Thomas Shank and John A. Nichols, 183–97. Kalamazoo, MI: Cistercian Publications.

Donovan, Vincent. 2003. *Christianity Rediscovered*. Maryknoll, NY: Orbis Books.

Dupuis, Jacques. 1997. *Toward a Christian Theology of Religious Pluralism*. Maryknoll, NY: Orbis Books.

Ellsberg, Robert. 1997. *All Saints: Daily Reflections on Saints, Prophets, and Witnesses for Our Time*. New York: Crossroad.

Eusebius. 1994. *Church History*. In *Nicene and Post-Nicene Fathers*, vol. 1, second series, ed. Philip Schaff and Henry Wace. Peabody, MA: Hendrickson Publishers.

Finch, Raymond. 2000. "Missionaries Today." *Origins* 30, no. 21 (2 November), 327–32.

Gittins, Anthony J. 1998. "Mission: What's It Got to Do with Me?" *The Living Light* 34, no. 3: 6–13.

Godin, Henri, and Yvan Daniel. 1943. *France, pays de mission?* Paris: Editions du Cerf.

Green, Michael. 1970. *Evangelism in the Early Church*. Grand Rapids, MI: Eerdmans.

Gutiérrez, Gustavo. 1993. *Las Casas: In Search of the Poor of Jesus Christ*. Maryknoll, NY: Orbis Books.

Irvin, Dale T., and Scott W. Sunquist. 2001. *History of the World Christian Movement*. Vol. 1, *Earliest Christianity to 1453*. Maryknoll, NY: Orbis Books.

Jenkins, Philip. 2002, *The Next Christendom: The Coming of Global Christianity*. Oxford: Oxford University Press.

Johnson, Luke Timothy. 1992. *The Acts of the Apostles*. Sacra Pagina 5. Collegeville, MN: The Liturgical Press.

Kilgallen, John J. 1989. "The Function of Stephen's Speech (Acts 7:2–53)." *Biblica* 70: 173–93.

Moffett, Samuel Hugh. 1992. *A History of Christianity in Asia*. Vol. 1, *Beginnings to 1500*. San Francisco: Harper Collins.

Neill, Stephen. 1964. *A History of Christian Missions*. London: Penguin Books.

Nguyen, Thanh van. 2004. *The Legitimation of the Gentile Mission and Integration: A Narrative Approach to Acts 10:1—11:18*. Doctoral dissertation, Gregorian University.

Norris, Frederick W. 2002. *Christianity: A Short Global History*. Oxford: One World.

Nothwehr, Dawn, ed. 2002. *Franciscan Theology of the Environment: An Introductory Reader.* Quincy, IL: Franciscan Press.

Palmer, Martin. 2001. *The Jesus Sutras: Rediscovering the Lost Scrolls of Taoist Christianity.* New York: Ballantine Wellspring.

Rahner, Karl. 1979. "Toward a Fundamental Theological Interpretation of Vatican II." *Theological Studies* 40: 716–27.

Reid, Barbara. 1997. "Women in the New Testament." In *Dictionary of Mission: Theology, History, Perspectives,* ed. Karl Müller, Theo Sundermeier, Stephen Bevans, and Richard Bliese, 480–90. Maryknoll, NY: Orbis Books.

Ruether, Rosemary, and Eleanor McLaughlin. 1979. *Women of Spirit: Female Leadership in the Jewish and Christian Traditions.* New York: Simon and Schuster.

Sanneh, Lamin. 1991. "The Yogi and the Commissar: Christian Missions and the African Response." *International Bulletin of Missionary Research* 15, no. 1: 2–11.

———. 2003. *Whose Religion Is Christianity?: The Gospel beyond the West.* Grand Rapids, MI: Eerdmans.

Schattauer, Thomas H., ed. 1999. *Inside Out: Worship in an Age of Mission.* Minneapolis, MN: Fortress Press.

Schreiter, Robert. 1992. *Reconciliation: Mission and Ministry in a Changing Social Order.* Maryknoll, NY: Orbis Books.

———. 1994. "Changes in Roman Catholic Attitudes toward Proselytism and Mission." In *New Directions in Mission and Evangelization 2,* ed. James A. Scherer and Stephen B. Bevans, 113–25. Maryknoll, NY: Orbis Books.

———. 1998. *The Ministry of Reconciliation: Spirituality and Strategies.* Maryknoll, NY: Orbis Books.

Schroeder, Roger. 2000. "Entering Someone Else's Garden: Cross-Cultural Mission/Ministry." In *The Healing Circle,* ed. Stephen Bevans, Eleanor Doidge, and Robert Schreiter, 147–61. Chicago: CCGM Publications.

Senior, Donald, and Carroll Stuhlmueller. 1983. *The Biblical Foundations for Mission.* Maryknoll, NY: Orbis Books.

Smith, Susan E. 2007. *Women in Mission: From the New Testament to Today.* Maryknoll, NY: Orbis Books.

Stark, Rodney. 1996. *The Rise of Christianity.* San Francisco: Harper Collins Publishers.

Tescaroli, Cirillo. n.d. *Daniel Comboni: A Pioneer of the Church in Africa.* Private publication by the Comboni Missionaries.

Thomas of Celano. 1972. "The First Life of St. Francis." In *St. Francis of Assisi, Writings and Early Biographies: English Omnibus of the Sources for the Life of St. Francis*, ed. Marion A. Habig, trans. Placid Hermann, 225–355. London: The Society for Promoting Christian Knowledge.

Tomko, Jozef Cardinal. 2001. "Mission for the Twenty-first Century: The Perspective of the Magisterium." In *Mission for the Twenty-first Century*, ed. Stephen Bevans and Roger Schroeder, 21–31. Chicago: CCGM Publications.

Truth, Sojourner. 1996. "Document 3: Sojourner Truth: The Conversion of a Female Slave." In Walls 1996.

Tshimika, Pakisa K., and Tim Lind. 2003. *Sharing Gifts in the Global Family of Faith: One Church's Experiment*. Intercourse, PA: Good Books.

United States Conference of Catholic Bishops. 1998. *Called to Global Solidarity: International Challenges for U.S. Parishes. A Statement of the National Conference of Catholic Bishops with Parish Resources*. Washington, DC: USCCB.

Walls, Andrew F. 1996. *The Missionary Movement in Christian History: Studies in the Transmission of the Faith*. Maryknoll, NY: Orbis Books.

———. 2002. *The Cross-Cultural Process in Christian History*. Maryknoll, NY: Orbis Books.

Yong, Amos. 2008. *Hospitality and the Other: Pentecost, Christian Practices, and the Neighbor*. Maryknoll, NY: Orbis Books.

Index